Wrestling with the Angel

Swarthmore Lecture 2001

Wrestling with the Angel

Quaker engagement in commercial and public affairs

Tony Stoller

Swarthmore Lecture 2001

QUAKER *Q* BOOKS

First published in July 2001 by Quaker Books
Friends House, Euston Road, London NW1 2BJ

http://www.quaker.org.uk

ISBN 0 85245 326 4

Design & typesetting: Jonathan Sargent
Printed and bound in Great Britain by Biddles Ltd
www.biddles.co.uk
Text typeface: Baskerville 10.5 on 14pt

Preface

The Swarthmore Lectureship was established by the Woodbrooke Extension Committee at a meeting held December 9, 1907: the minute of the Committee providing for an 'annual lecture on some subject relating to the message and work of the Society of Friends'. The name Swarthmore was chosen in memory of the home of Margaret Fox, which was always open to the earnest seeker after Truth, and from which loving words of sympathy and substantial material help were sent to fellow workers.

The lectureship has a twofold purpose: first, to interpret to the members of the Society of Friends their message and mission; and secondly, to bring before the public the spirit, the aims and fundamental principles of Friends. The lecturers alone are responsible for any opinions expressed.

The lectureship provides both for the publication of a book and for the delivery of a lecture, the latter usually at the time of assembly of Britain Yearly Meeting of the Society of Friends. A lecture related to the present book was delivered at Yearly Meeting in Exeter on the evening of July 30, 2001.

Dedication

For Andy, Juliette and Tim

Contents

'[Jacob] rose up that night...and passed over the ford Jabbok....And Jacob was left alone; and there wrestled a man with him until the breaking of the day. And when he saw that he prevailed not against him, he touched the hollow of his thigh; and the hollow of Jacob's thigh was out of joint, as he wrestled with him. And he said, Let me go, for the day breaketh. And he said, I will not let thee go, except thou bless me.'

Genesis 32: 22

'That same night Jacob got up...and crossed the River Jabbok...Then a man came and wrestled with him until just before daybreak. When the man saw that he was not winning the struggle, he struck Jacob on the hip, and it was thrown out of joint. The man said "Let me go; daylight is coming". "I won't unless you bless me", Jacob answered.'

Good News Bible

1 Introduction

A review of the themes and challenges of the book and lecture

Fenit in County Kerry is a self-consciously prosaic and practical harbour amid the impossible romanticism of Tralee Bay. We talked admiringly with a local yachtsman there, as the wind blew fierce drizzle at us over the Benagh mountain massif from the Atlantic, about the dangers of Kerry Head and the Shannon Estuary, compared with the manicured waters of the Solent. He observed that 'everyone has a Cape Horn on their doorstep'.

I am setting out in this book, and the Swarthmore Lecture, to navigate the waters around my own Cape Horn. That is to say, I am going to consider my own experience of commerce, and the world of public administration, and consider what general questions and implications arise for Quakers, both individuals and the Religious Society as a whole.

So what have been my own areas of experience? A post-war baby-boomer, on the non-Zionist fringe of the north London Jewish community, I followed through my early interest in Quakerism by first attending and then becoming a member of the Religious Society through Newbury Preparative Meeting in 1984. Among Quakers, I have been a PM elder, and currently serve on the Quaker Communications Central Committee. I judge that our Quakerism is at its essence a practical, proletarian mysticism. In my working life I have pinballed between the commercial worlds of newspapers, radio and retailing, and public administration in the regulation of broadcasting.

When I began to chart a course for this lecture, I was quickly given two starting points. The first was a conviction that most Quakers, and Quakerism as a whole, have become too disengaged from the realities of day-to-day life as they present themselves both in business and in the way in which we are governed. I intended therefore from the start to argue that greater engagement with the commercial and public worlds was an obligation on us and on our institutions. As I have researched my topic, and gained from the wisdom of Friends with whom I have discussed it, I have come to understand that there is much more individual engagement of this sort around than I had realised. However, I have not been dissuaded from my first central thesis, that taken as a whole we do much less than we could and indeed much less than we should, as a consequence of a reluctance to enter into commercial and political enterprise.

Second, I wanted to reflect on the implications for a Quaker individual of engaging in such a manner. The image I have begun with, and which accompanies me through this book and lecture, is of Jacob wrestling with the Angel. The old testament patriarch was not above a bit of sharp practice or two to augment his flocks, but when push came to shove he was able to engage with a force beyond his strength, staying locked with it and being at the end both wounded and blessed by it. The 'Angel'[1] can stand here for any challenge which presents itself as something forbidding, unfamiliar and potent, which – if we have the strength – we may confront and thereby achieve much, but at the likely cost of personal damage; or from which we may feel we have to withdraw, lest we are over-mastered. The story of Jacob and the Angel as a whole serves to illustrate what may be the implications when we engage with the realities of the modern world, in the terms of the society in which we now live.

It may seem to us at times the outcome of such engagement is that we are only undefeated because we have gone on trying. However, I believe that the very fact of continued engagement with the mainstream of secular society – working within it and where necessary challenging it on its own terms – is an essential part of our witness, and the work we do whilst so engaged is valid service. Further, by remaining both engaged and evidently so, we can have at least as much beneficial effect as those outside the system who challenge or criticise it. At best, it will be the partnership of the engaged and the critics which will achieve the most. I began with the view that our Religious Society generally needs to give more than passing recognition to the value of work done within the wider secular society, as it does more willingly to service given in our currently more traditional areas of activity. I have tested that first impression, and find that it stands the test.

I start then with these twin themes: that we need Quaker individuals who are more engaged with commerce and public affairs; and that we need to renew the partnership between such engaged Friends and those who are active in more caring or spiritual fields, if we are to maintain our full witness and offer the best service to society. In the first half of this work, after some scoping and definitions (in chapter 2), I will offer examples of both those aspects, looking first at examples of issues – modern and historical – for Quakers in business and commercial life (chapter 3), and then at public administration and the state (chapter 4). I will then try and draw out how we could change the way in which we conduct our own enterprises, to achieve effective engagement (chapter 5) and how we and others present ideas to a wider world (chapter 6). In what is intended to be the heart of my argument, I consider how to give effect to spiritual values in the secular world for individuals (chapter 7) and for our Religious Society as a whole (chapter 8). I realise that some readers might want to start with the principles before considering practical examples; my own journey has gone from the examples towards the conclusions, and that is how I set it out here.

The subject as a whole raises a series of questions, which accompany us on our way through the topic:

◆ what issues face a Quaker in business or public life, which go beyond those posed for people of goodwill generally?
◆ to what extent are the 'assumed' responses to such issues to be relied upon? and how far can we be justified in substituting our judgement for what will produce the best outcome to replace those normative views?
◆ can and should we expect a greater level of engagement from Quakers as individuals, and from the Religious Society as a whole?
◆ what degree of support is an engaged individual entitled to expect from the Religious Society? and what might be done to enhance the support which is currently available?
◆ by what standards should a Quaker conduct himself or herself, when engaged in this way?
◆ and, what techniques from the wider world could or should usefully be adopted in our own Quaker enterprises?

I want to encourage Quaker individuals and Quaker institutions to engage with commercial and political life, as well as with the more usual challenges of, for example, education and healthcare. I believe that we can and should establish a 'partnership' between commercially/politically informed Friends, and those within the caring professions. This would enable the whole Religious Society to work to wrestle with the Angel which is everyday life, and also more narrowly to operate more effectively and inclusively itself.

If this is to happen, we will need to find a place for those engaged in these fields alongside the experience, attitudes and preconceptions of the caring professions which so dominate our Religious Society. If we cannot, then we risk also diminishing the value of the type of work with which so many of us feel more comfortable, because it will be done less well than it could be, and with diminishing relevance. However, if we can include *engagement* alongside what were our late twentieth century preoccupations – and we can do it if we want to – that will be to the immense benefit of our effective witness and service.

Note to Chapter 1

1 The story has become known as 'Jacob and the Angel', and that indeed is the title Sir Jacob Epstein gave to his statue, now on display in the Tate Britain Gallery in London, which is shown on the cover of this book. Strictly speaking, the Hebrew of the Bible is silent about the identity of the being whom Jacob engaged, calling him אִישׁ (which as the Authorised Version translates means simply 'a man'). However, there is little difficulty in identifying the 'man' as divine from the name he gave Jacob; 'Israel', one who has wrestled with God. And the Authorised Version goes on to say that 'Jacob called the name of the place Peniel: for I have seen God face to face, and my life is preserved'.

2   Cheating the Prophet

Scope, definitions and context

To begin this exploration, I need to establish its scope. In this chapter, therefore, I will offer some definitions, and that will also involve setting some fairly arbitrary limits on the topics to be included. After that, and some issues that it will provoke, I will consider whether Quaker participation in the wider world is unacceptable *per se*. I will conclude with a brief look at what many commentators assume is a fast-changing world, to judge whether the principles that we have established in the past may be undermined by a rather different future.

Words and meanings

My subject is the inter-related worlds of business and public affairs, and I intend to describe this nexus by the shorthand of the 'commercial state'. I am using that phrase to encompass both the business and commercial world as a whole, and the arena of politics, administration and public affairs. In doing so, I am intending to be generally inclusive. For instance, I am not concerned only with major companies, rather than individual enterprise. Many of the issues facing those who work in or deal with major multinationals are much the same – in essence if not in scale – as those arising from smaller companies. Many also

6

apply in the institutions of the care sector. However, my own experience encompasses public administration and commercial companies but not the industrial or social sectors, unlike the historic Quaker experience which encompassed both. So I must stay with what I know.

I also have to draw a line (which I admit is a fairly fuzzy one) and leave outside those 'alternative' enterprises which inevitably raise rather different issues at a practical, day-to-day level. We all greatly value Quaker enterprises and other alternatives to the western capital-based model of the late twentieth and early twenty-first centuries. They have much to offer, both in themselves and as ideas which can be read across into the modern established western world. But, although many of the issues in mainstream commercial life find echoes (and sometimes, indeed, resolutions) in alternative models for business enterprise, that separate culture is a vast topic which needs to be considered in its own right. Sadly, I have neither the space nor time to do so here.

Similarly, I will regard mainstream politics and established public administration as being inside my 'commercial state' focus, with direct action or other power cores lying outside, although relevant to this exercise for the light they may throw. Where the distinction becomes more difficult to maintain is in what might be called the 'public enterprise'. Thus, the UK's National Health Service is probably the largest single employer in Europe, and it has an integral if uneasy relationship with the pharmaceutical industry. As a further example among many, schools are having to adopt many of the techniques of commercial management, and endure the effects of the market intruding into what most of us had hoped was a market-free zone.

Whether or not these 'public enterprises', and the increasing market pressures felt in the caring professions generally, bring them within the 'commercial state' can remain moot. The key point is that commerce and public affairs increasingly fit together into a single nexus, and that they represent an area of activity in which Friends were once closely involved, but are now much less so. They offer challenges and dilemmas, and thus also examples and precepts, which are of even wider application. So a study of the 'commercial state' as I have defined it here ought also to be of direct value in the areas of 'public enterprise' which are increasingly drawn into this arena. Certainly, the pressures on individual Friends in, for example, health jobs or within the criminal justice system, are no less – and often no different – from those which are manifest in the 'commercial state' areas. They, too, wrestle with these particular Angels.

However, I still sense a distinction felt among Friends between the 'commercial state' of business and government on the one hand, and 'personal concerns' of the caring professions on the other, as if there were a difference between getting our hands dirty in commerce and administration, contrasted with morally 'safe' jobs and personal good actions and intentions. The vast majority of Quakers are either involved in the latter group in both instances, or are retired (usually from that same area) and value the quieter virtues. If they are no longer active participants, it is my experience that they nevertheless applaud, quietly, those who seek to stand apart from the 'commercial state', and particularly those who engage in direct action against it from outside, yet often feel uncomfortable with the ideas, trends and even the people who remain engaged with it from within. That discomfort is accentuated as the influence of the 'commercial state' invades 'public enterprises'. The cumulative effect is to give our Religious Society a bias against the commercial and political world that is the complete opposite of where we were at the end of the nineteenth century, and to make Quakerism less welcoming and less effective than it could be. It also too often denies us a partnership between those working in these different fields which could offer much of value to us and in those areas where we seek to have effect.

My use of the word 'engagement', which runs throughout the text, is also intended to reflect this distinction, which I think

Friends generally perceive. I intend it in the special sense of *engagement with the commercial state,* and at a level or in a role where it is possible to have some influence on policy and practice. A special use of a common word is necessary, because I know it would be nonsense to talk about 'taking part in the real world', since the arenas of business and public life are no more or less 'real' than any other sector. I also realise that Friends tackling the immense current problems of the public sector are themselves fully engaged, wrestling as it were with Angels of their own. I hope they will forgive me appropriating, for the purpose of this lecture, the word 'engagement' to mean what I want it to mean.

When I talk about Quakers as a whole in our organised form, I will write of the 'Religious Society', to help distinguish this from society at large. This is deliberately imprecise. I deprecate but acknowledge the obsession which we have developed over recent years with structures, names, and acronyms. For that reason I will avoid speaking of 'Britain Yearly Meeting', unless I mean the event itself, even though it is primarily to that Yearly Meeting that this work is addressed. For work which is undertaken under the auspices of Friends House, collectively on behalf of British Quakers, I will write of our 'corporate work'. The phrase is not mine, but is the one in current usage. It is also a phrase which highlights the link between commercial enterprise and social action, and as such already hints at some of the ideas which I will advance. For particular Quaker projects, in all their diversity, I will write of 'Quaker enterprises'.

I will also generally use the word 'employer' when I consider the position and challenges facing those Friends who, either as managers or as proprietors, have people working for them in a commercial or public organisation. When the main such undertakings concerning us were Quaker businesses, in the eighteenth and nineteenth centuries, then a Quaker employer was a particular animal. Nowadays, the term can be used much more loosely, to indicate the 'boss'. It is incidentally most usual for the boss now also to be an employee, which is one of the characteristics distinguishing our commercial society from the heyday of the Quaker industrialists, and which can help to bridge the supposed divide between employer and employee.

Commercial and public life

Joining business and public affairs is convenient for my purpose here. However, the link goes deeper than that. The close identification between the two is evident in so many ways, and that can present just the type of dilemma which is my concern. For example, increasingly, staff at both junior and senior levels move from one sector to the other, raising questions for us as they go. On what terms may a public official move into the commercial sector for which he has been taking, say, a regulatory responsibility? I have made the move both ways, from the broadcasting regulator, the Independent Broadcasting Authority, to running one of its franchised radio stations; and more recently from retailing back into regulation. I know that there need to be rules, fair to the public interest and also to the individual. A concerned Quaker may well feel they have a part to play in helping to frame and police those rules. Yet such rules may well be drawn up with one eye on possible legal challenge and the other on public opinion, leaving little attention to spare for what might objectively be thought 'right'. Against what standards can an individual set their own, personal rules on such an issue?

The link between business and public affairs is deeper and closer still. In *Ruling Britannia*, Andrew Marr tartly observes that 'any account of the British constitution today which omits to mention the refreshment tent at the Stella Artois tennis tournament, as well as Prime Minister's question time; or the good seats at Covent Garden as well as the good seats on the government benches, is a little naïve.'[1] I have no doubt that many arrangements are made, difficulties eased, and ideas floated in the course of corporate entertainment involving business people and officials.

There are hospitality tents at Scientific Congresses serving the same purposes.

Once again, for the concerned individual a dilemma arises. If I am entertained with tickets to the opera, is this simply part of building a good and friendly relationship with those that I am regulating? They do not expect to 'buy' my good opinion of them, and provided there are clear and public rules about what may be accepted and what may not, it would be 'received opinion' that little harm can result. Indeed, to refuse too often can not only give offence, but also create a distance and sense of mistrust which can often make taking the harsh decision actually more difficult. Yet I know that, at some stage during the evening, either the host or another guest is likely to have 'just a quiet word' about one problem or another. Is that good, or an abuse? At another level, are the 'toffs' in the opera box exploiting a privilege of wealth and influence which is to the detriment of other people, even the majority? Yet if we so judge, and take a moral position to avoid such contact, will not the decisions which are made, eased or usefully held back on such occasions be taken without our participation, which might possibly have influenced them for good? My point is that these new forms are not just of academic interest. They are real issues for anyone who wishes to stay engaged.

Commercial 'contamination'?
There is a central point which I must address before I go any further. It was best illustrated for me by discussion among a group of Friends with whom, as a Committee for Clearness, I had been considering this lecture. One Friend said that it was important not to look on the involvement of commercial issues in Quaker concerns as a 'regrettable contamination'; another, that such a contamination is precisely what happens whenever the practices of the market are imported into social or public affairs. I imagine that this dichotomy will exist among Quakers at large. It is not to be

resolved, but it needs to be explored.

The belief that commercial practice is anathema arises, I judge, from two near-contemporary causes. The first is that too much business practice in the greed years of the 1980s harked back to the worst excesses of capitalism, the unfeeling exploitation of individuals for private profit. The second is the importation into areas previously untouched by 'the market', such as education and health, of notions which supposedly represent normal commercial behaviour. There is some validity in both of these worries, but not in the end enough in either to justify a refusal to engage.

Some Friends take the view that ingrained in business is the exploitation of staff, customers and the resources of the world. In my experience, as a generalisation that is a fallacy. The reality of working (or managing) in business is usually reasonably congenial. For instance, the growth of employment protection and other legislation ensures that there is little bad behaviour in the large majority of companies, if it were anyway likely. With the growth of managers who are also employees, the gulf between employer and staff is much reduced. So also, increased environmental pressures and awareness, encouraged by the rise of ethical considerations in investment, make companies more socially aware than ever before. That is not by any means to say that all is well. However, my direct experience – and that of Friends and others with whom I have tested this point – is that business these days is much more likely to behave well in most respects than is the public or voluntary sector. The abuses of Ofsted would not long have been endured in most of the commercial world.

However, a good number of bad practices seem to have migrated from the commercial to the state sector in the 1990s. The bizarre concept of an 'internal market' in the Health Service, for example, owed little to how markets actually work in business. I remain amazed that there are those who continue to believe (or at least to argue) that free markets inevitably produce public good. There is, it seems, a view that markets left to operate untrammelled are somehow benign. We know from both experience and theory that the opposite is true, that even in widget-manufacture free markets tend to monopoly and exploitation of the public, while in areas of legitimate public policy interest they can be positively malign. That is why in practice commercial markets are highly regulated.

As one example, routine appraisal is not a stick with which you seek to beat staff, as it is perceived to be among many teachers, but an essential part of how good companies manage and develop staff through clear objectives and honest assessment. It is not the use of such techniques, borrowed from the commercial world, which is the problem. It is their misuse, arising from misunderstanding and misapplication. Importing into the caring sector the false concept of a 'benign market' is the sort of thing which gives business a bad name.

I am confident in rejecting the notion that it would be a contamination to urge more interplay between the 'commercial state' and our Quakerly concerns. Indeed, I am setting out to demonstrate the opposite, that both we and that 'commercial state' itself will greatly benefit from greater interaction.

In this text, therefore, I am setting out to correct some of the common misapprehensions among Quakers about the relevance of the 'commercial state' and its techniques. I am not seeking to derogate the social, voluntary or ethical worlds, but to argue first that there is an equal validity in both, and second that we need to look to the repair of the bridge between them so that two-way traffic can resume its full flow.

In doing so, we will not escape the feeling that we are involved – from time to time – in matters which compromise our 'purity'. If I had any doubt about the need to wrestle with this particular Angel regardless, they are set aside by Dietrich Bonhoeffer. 'If any man tries to escape guilt in responsibility, he detaches himself from the ultimate reality of human existence...He sets his own personal conscience above responsibility for men, and he is blind to the more irredeemable guilt which he incurs.'[2]

Future shock?

I am writing this in the last months of the year 2000. Yet I intend to begin exploring the challenges and dilemma of the 'commercial state' by considering events of April 1869. As I write that, I can sense the modernists recoil. Surely, they will say, our society is changing so fast that even ideas drawn from the present day are going to be outmoded in no time at all. By way of concluding this introduction, therefore, I want to look briefly at some examples of factors bearing upon the 'commercial state' which futurists argue are likely to change it, and whether that should modify any conclusions drawn from the examination that follows in later chapters.

In his fantasy, *The Napoleon of Notting Hill*, G.K. Chesterton wrote that the human race has played at children's games from the beginning, 'and one of the games to which it is most attached is called "Keep tomorrow dark" and is also named "Cheat the Prophet". The players listen very carefully and respectfully to all that the clever men have to say about what is to happen in the next generation. The players then wait until all the clever men are dead, and bury them nicely. Then they go and do something else. That is all. For a race of simple tastes, however, it is great fun.'[3]

'Cheat the prophet' is still a most popular pastime. We hardly need, for example, to try and guess the nature of the new technologies, because in practice they exist alongside established technologies for years and years. The Internet was invented in 1969, so its rate of take-up is about the same as that applying to most new electronic hardware, from the refrigerator to the video machine (whatever its proponents may wish you to believe). Moore's law, beloved by the modernisers, states (correctly) that in recent years the capacity of computer chips has doubled every eighteen months while their price halves. It does not assert – how could it? – that we all immediately acquire items using only the new chips and discontinue using anything else. The demise of the printed book has been confidently predicted. However, I think we may conclude that, at the very least, the book is safe for now and for a long future. The 'paperless office' is usually, at least in my experience, anything but paperless. And technologies are in any event less enduring than ethics and morality.

That is the point. Whatever trends are evident in society as a whole, the ethical issues are at root the same. Thus we may note that to an even greater extent than before, business is now dependent upon the intelligence it has at its disposal, brain replacing brawn even in heavy industry. In Ford's Atlanta car plant it now requires only 17 hours of direct labour to produce a car.[4] Intelligent machines, and the intelligent people who design and operate them do the rest. Intelligent people therefore may become the most precious commercial asset. Thus, if we are to wrestle with this new manifestation of the business Angel, we still need to know the principle by which we will deal with and treat people.

The centrality of intelligence in business life is certainly changing the position of many individuals. Since a company doesn't own someone else's intelligence, the best it can hope for is to rent it for a while. This means that the relationship between key worker and employer changes, and a new set of practical dilemmas arise, such as over the ownership of intellectual property developed while working for one company and the right of a worker to move between employers. Particular skill sets become more quickly outdated, adding to the striking disappearance of the 'job for life', which was the most characteristic feature of employment in the immediate past, a most unsettling feature for those of us who grew up in an earlier age. By contrast though, intelligence (unlike, say, coal) is not used up when it is once used. Its development by one employer, through training, adds permanently to the wealth of that industry and society as a whole. This poses new challenges for the employer and the employee, but it does not change the basic morality of obligations under which each operates.

That applies also to consumers. Leadbetter illustrates the nature of this change by suggesting that Delia Smith rather than Adam Smith better illustrates the economics of the current world order. 'When we consume knowledge – a recipe for example – we do not possess it. The recipe remains Delia Smith's; indeed, that is why we use it. By buying her book we have bought access to the recipes within it. Ownership of the recipe is in effect shared between Delia and the millions of users.'[5] But the judgement over what resources it is appropriate to consume, or share, is at root the same one as when buying manufactured goods. The principle, say, of giving fair measure is no different.

Within our times in work, genuine job satisfaction becomes a more real prospect for more people as the assembly lines and their like are run more by robot machines. Despite the computer screen, our expectations for the quality of working life for ourselves and for others can be higher. Suddenly, a chance arises for an 'industrial mission' not just concerned with alleviating harsh physical conditions but with the real prospect of adding to the quality of people's lives in work as much as out. Set against that, the sense of identity which we acquire from our work is increasingly threatened by its comparative impermanence. This is not just a dinner-party characteristic. Even Quakers are apt to ask 'what do you do?' as a way of identifying a stranger. We can no longer rely on the personal security and identity that comes from a job title. Therefore the need to establish a new basis on which to become engaged in the wider business or administrative world becomes even more important. 'I'm just writing computer programmes until I become a famous novelist' is no basis for a sense of belonging. Finding a new location for loyalty in the 'commercial state' may help ease the sense of rootlessness and alienation surprisingly evident even among those who might be thought to have a stake in society, helping them in turn to assist better those who are genuinely excluded.

We can assume with a fair degree of confidence the main

factors for the commercial world over the next twenty years or so (barring major nuclear or environmental catastrophe or disastrous epidemics). The effects of population growth will be manageable for a generation, thanks to technological advances. Although the rate of technological discovery has been frantic, the time-lag between the invention of a technology and its widespread adoption by consumers is such that we already have around us, at least in their early stages, the main technologies which will affect us for the next twenty years. Any rules we establish for engaging with the society they create now will serve for a while yet.

We also know that the pressures of disorder which affect us now will be with us for some time to come. Some economists acknowledge that societies experiencing a burst of economic growth endure – and usually accept – a fair degree of corruption and lawlessness in the process. The American Wild West is probably a more familiar example than the present state of Russia, the former having been comfortably mythologised by Hollywood. However, 'enduring prosperity requires societies which are stable, ordered and honest'.[6] Football hooliganism (on and off the pitch), vandalism, laddism and misogyny, 'sink estates' and commercial sleaze threaten both our comfort of mind and the well-being of our societies. The economist will argue that 'ordinary people have to want to sustain the balance between order and individualism which leads to societies which are both efficient and humane.'[7] For Quakers, the equation is less simple. What balance do we want, and how can we set about achieving it? It is my thesis that we cannot do this from outside the 'system', but only by playing an active part in it.

And what about the Internet, which some people would have us believe is the greatest agent for change since the invention of printing, maybe even of the wheel itself? Some of the current claims are obviously wide of the mark. In her 2000 Reith Lecture[8] Dr Gro Harlem Brundtland foresaw the Internet being a great equaliser giving everyone access to the same information about health care. Yet in the same speech she said that of the world's 6 billion people, 3 billion survive on less than $2 a day, and 1.3 billion on less than $1 per day. These two statements are irreconcilable when applied to the present state of the world. Given that seventy per cent of the world's population have never used a telephone, and ninety-five per cent have never used a computer, it may be reasonable to conclude that in our present state the world has more urgent access issues confronting it than the ability to surf the Internet.

For the purpose of this lecture, the Internet is significant because it heightens issues and points up dilemmas which are endemic in the operation of the modern 'commercial state'. The speed of electronic communication means that judgements need to be made much quicker. In my daily work, if I am pressed to give a faster answer, am I more likely to give the expedient rather than the proper reply? Do we really achieve greater openness by making huge amounts of data available to the Internet-capable, or just the illusion of openness? How can we cope with the gulf that has already opened between the information-rich and the information-poor, of which the figures in the previous paragraph are evidence? If there is a surge in Internet-based home shopping, what will be the impact on transport and distribution, with their ecological implications? If we are to contribute to the resolution of these and so many similar issues, we will need to be part of the process. That means that Quakers will have to be engaged with the making of commercial and policy decisions. The changes in the way we live now make that more necessary than ever.

In the administrative and political world, a new pattern of governance has emerged over the past thirty years. One key feature in Britain has been the centralising of political power towards an executive authority. The erosion of the scope and influence of local government, as its powers are shifted to Westminster, have been followed by a weakening of the influence of Parliament in favour of the executive. Ministerial and even cabinet authority diminish, as effective party and national management is seen to require core decision-making to be carried through by the centralists alone. However, the centre cannot do everything, even if it seeks to control (or at least influence) everything. So as the traditional outposts of governance have power taken away from them, they are replaced by other centres of devolved authority such as regulators, the statutory corporations, and the so-called 'quangocracy'. Traditional local authorities were elected and were thus more or less accountable, however imperfectly. The new bodies are appointed not elected, requiring an elaborate system of accountability and other safeguards to be constructed for them.

There is nothing necessarily wrong in the centralised state with its devolved executive. The old decentralised state had hardly produced a society or economy to be proud of. As a regulator and therefore quangocrat myself, I know both the virtues and the potential pitfalls of this type of governance. However, it is inescapably different from the model that most Quakers have in mind when they think of the state. If we want to influence for good how we are governed, then it is with the realities of this new world that we have to engage, not the nostalgia of the old.

I will look in the fourth chapter of this book at how this may be done successfully. The examples there of Transport 2000 and Jubilee 2000 illustrate how the new politics requires and forges new alliances, how the previous traditionalists become radicals and challenge the once radical new conservatives. In this world, I will argue that our established Quaker routes for social and political action need to be re-examined. In doing so, we need also to reflect on some of the techniques used by the new politics. I have written previously of the 'opera box lobby'. Just as challenging for us is the relationship between presentation and substance. In a 'commercial state' where information is the prime raw material on which intelligence, the key skill, must work, the ownership and presentation of information by governments is a fundamental issue. This is not just the question of 'spin', which I will consider in chapter 6.

It means that we have to question who owns information. As I write, Parliament has largely abandoned its original impulse for meaningful Freedom of Information legislation, but the Human Rights Act will establish the right of access to information and the limits allowed to the state in acquiring it. This is not just a matter of being able to see your own medical records or credit-rating. It will go to the heart of the individual's ability to participate in governance and the decision-making processes, confirming for each citizen the right to receive and impart information. With widespread uncertainty at all levels, we who are concerned about society have a real chance to participate in and influence the outcome in this key area. We need to know what we think, and have both the skill and channels to express that.

If as Quaker individuals or Quaker institutions we operate only outside the 'commercial state', we will lose a major opportunity of access and influence. If we only dissent, then we lose not only access but also the right to participate in the making and interpreting of policy. If we reject any involvement in the materialism of the 'commercial state', then we are excluding ourselves, our ideas and our service from areas where they might have effect; yet those are areas central to the way in which we live and our society functions. If on the other hand we are prepared to contemplate a partnership between those who are involved with the 'commercial state' and those who are outside it, then we can feel a renewed confidence about meeting those opportunities and obligations. I am not prepared to shirk this task, to refuse to wrestle with this Angel, and I do not want our Religious Society to absent itself either.

Notes to Chapter 2

1 Andrew Marr *Ruling Britannia* Michael Joseph 1995 p 252
2 Dietrich Bonhoeffer *Ethics* SCM Press 1955 p 210
3 G.K. Chesterton *The Napoleon of Notting Hill* Penguin Modern Classics p 9
4 Charles Handy *The Empty Raincoat* Arrow Business Books 1995 p 23
5 Charles Leadbetter *Living on Thin Air* Penguin Books 2000 p 32
6 Hamish McCrea *The World in 2020* HarperCollins 1995 p 265
7 Ibid.
8 Gro Harlem Brundtland *Respect for the Earth – BBC Reith Lectures 2000* Profile Books 2000 p 50

3   The chocolate spies

Dilemmas for Quakers in business and commercial life

In April of 1869, Friends at Fisher Street Meeting in Carlisle received a letter of resignation from the biscuit-maker J.D. Carr and his wife Jane. It was a simple and gentle letter, uncritical and modest. The Carrs had seen their two sons, Henry and James, disowned from membership by the Meeting for having defied marriage rules and being seen 'in another place where paid ministry is employed'. Now they themselves were leaving.

'It was a time of agonising significance in J.D.'s life', wrote Margaret Forster. 'His entire career, which had been so enormously successful and had made him, in Carlisle, an important and wealthy man, had been founded upon and guided by Quaker principles. His religion, and his worship within it, was the cornerstone of all his work. Take it away, and what would happen?'[1]

J.D.'s dilemma is in one way entirely contemporary. His (and Jane Carr's) personal agonisings over membership are something we are familiar with in our own Meetings, and often in our own consciences, even if the drama of Victorian Quakerism's disownments are thankfully left in the historic past. But the context of a successful Quaker businessman finding his business so closely interwoven with his Quakerism is largely foreign to us. That is our loss, and society's too.

In this chapter I will be looking at a series of dilemmas which

22

confront those Quakers who do choose to engage with business and commercial life. I intend to use them to illustrate the broader question about how one can stay engaged with this part of modern life, especially in view of the culture of criticism of wealth-producing activities which is so prevalent in our Religious Society. I am not attempting to be comprehensive in covering all possible issues. That would need a long textbook, which this is certainly not. Rather I will use examples of issues in a range of fields which I hope will represent the topic as a whole. Those will cover the extent to which general business methods may be adopted by Quakers in business, and how the Quaker as employer should deal with employment and personnel issues. At the heart of this chapter will be consideration of the creation of wealth through business enterprise; and I will conclude with some observations on ethical investment and how such ethical principles translate into business generally.

J.D. Carr, by the way, found that 'something had gone out of his life: that certainty he had always had as a Quaker had vanished and he missed it.'[2]

Joseph Rowntree's chocolate factory

There is little other than the matter of scale which separates large and small business enterprises when it comes to issues of principle, practice and ethics. Henry Isaac Rowntree's chocolate business in 1861 employed one salesman and a dozen workers, and had an annual turnover of only £1,000. When Joseph Rowntree joined his brother in 1869 prospects were still uncertain. After tightening up the bookkeeping, a good Quaker skill, and thus avoiding the threat of bankruptcy, a great Quaker shame, Joseph embarked on some rather unquakerly industrial espionage. It was, as Walvin remarks, 'a development which fell some way short of the elevated ideals of Quaker business conduct.'[3]

Rowntree advertised in the London press for workers and a foreman 'who thoroughly understands the manufacture of Rock

and other Cocoas, confection and other chocolates'. He then
questioned applicants about the processes used by their current
employers, taking full notes and paying his informants if they
handed over to him production recipes. The process was so successful that Rowntree moved on to approach employees from
other companies directly. Walvin records that 'he talked to Cadbury's
workers in Birmingham and was by now making regular visits to
London to buy trade secrets. He always paid, but the sums were
small for such valuable information. His archives contain a report
of a payment of £3.'

So what? No one, not even a Quaker, is immune from bad
practice. That is not my point. What these events indicate is one
of the ways in which Joseph Rowntree was able to turn an ailing
business into a major and successful company. Rowntree was one
of the famous roll-call of Quaker enterprise in the eighteenth and
nineteenth centuries – Barclay, Cadbury, Carr, Corbyn, Darby, Fry,
Gurney, Hanbury, Huntley and Palmers, Reckitts, Taylor, Tuke,
Were. It is widely agreed that 'Quaker wealth was used...to pursue
the decency which lay at the heart of Quaker social thought'.[4]
Sound goods and fair dealing, fixed prices and honest services,
honourable agreements and a word to be trusted, laid the
foundation for successful trading. Yet even in that context, the
methods of his time commended themselves even to such as
Joseph Rowntree.

The nature of the dilemma, then as now, for Quakers in business is clear. In many ways, perhaps most, you can carry on your
business to high standards, setting an example to other traders
and to customers. That benefits you. It also benefits society as a
whole since the emulation of good practice, if it is also commer-
cially successful, is a far more effective means of lifting the
principled level of any activity than, say, law or regulation. Yet
you cannot use exclusively 'noble' means. To survive in the harsh
trading environment, and to remain engaged with commerce,
there may be times when you will need to adopt other less rep-

utable techniques. Is that acceptable? Is it fair to claim, not so much that the end justifies the means (always a suspect claim), but that paying the price to remain engaged is better than leaving the field to those who will make just as much use of the doubtful practices but little if any of the worthy ones? Should we wrestle with the Angel, or decline the match?

Jonathan Dale in a previous Swarthmore Lecture[5] has cautioned that our view of the achievements of the Victorian Quaker industrialists might be rose-tinted. However, while it is certainly unrealistic to regard even the founders of the great Quaker trusts as erstwhile saints, it is probably equally wide of the mark to assume that any contact with Mammon automatically defiles any enterprise. Dale himself writes that, in his view, those who work in a materialist world find themselves 'infiltrated by secular values' and then goes on to suggest that those secular values include fiddling your tax returns, defrauding insurance companies, supporting the 'black economy'.[6] Now there is no doubt about the potential of every individual to behave badly. Most of us have done things which would not stand scrutiny even by ourselves. There is every prospect of that happening while we are engaged with the 'commercial state'; but there is equally plenty of opportunity for behaving badly when we are not.

I do not recognise the notion that only those in 'pure' occupations will avoid the venality of daily life. That applies not only to Quakers but equally for the vast majority of the carefully honest people I work and have worked with, in a range of business and administrative enterprises. Pure behaviour is not the preserve of the non-commercial, nor venality the exclusive habit of the commercial. Even Jonathan Dale's offered mitigation that 'integrity from the sidelines is too easy'[7] misses the point. It is no easier from the sidelines than from the centre of the court. It is actually difficult everywhere. The problem here is that a good many among us assume that corruption marks all aspects of commercial life, without justification and perhaps even without acknowledging that we do so. Yet those assumptions demean working people. They also damage the Religious Society itself, because they exclude us from the active participation in central aspects of life as it is lived by most people.

Equal opportunities in employment

Writing in *The Spectator*, Martin Mears has described how the Crown Prosecution Service itself was found guilty of victimisation and racial discrimination by the Bedford Employment Tribunal.[8] The case as reported centred upon a decision by the CPS not to promote one of its lawyers, a black woman with a history of sensitivity on these issues. The decision was made by a 'balanced board' of three people, with a female chair and an ethnic minority member. The applicant was alleged to have had only a moderate record, and the CPS had taken careful steps to employ a fair marking system of assessment. In short, as reported it seems that the employer had done all that could have been expected of it. Nevertheless, the Tribunal found that there had been both direct and indirect discrimination and awarded the applicant £38,000 in compensation, which included £30,000 for injury to feelings.

This case seems to depict a sequence of events which every employer dreads. The experience of accusations of racial prejudice, made by those who are either unsuccessful in their applications for jobs or have been subject to disciplinary procedures, is depressingly a common one.

What can a Quaker employer do to combat racial prejudice in the workplace? I guess that all of us in the position to make employment judgements probably wish to err on the side of positive discrimination. We are keenly aware of the injustices suffered by black people in our workforce over many years, and would like to redress the balance by providing opportunities. That is not always easy to do. Race relations experts speak of the 'chill factor', where members of minority groups can feel uncomfortable even in the absence of any discrimination because of the strength of the host culture. In areas of work where very few ethnic minority members are seen to work, it can be difficult for that reason alone to get the applications from which to make a balanced choice. We need to take steps, and be seen to do so, to make it clear that applying is a credible and realistic option for people from such groups, as well as ensuring that in the workplace itself they are treated fairly and with understanding.

Then an issue like the Bedford Tribunal arises. We could usefully reflect on what a Quaker employer might do in such circumstances. The potential bad publicity of fighting a tribunal case can be damaging for an organisation, and wounding for the individuals concerned. Should different employment judgements have been made? Should, for example, the CPS have promoted someone they did not feel was the best candidate in order to avoid the risk of challenge? Should they have settled the eventual case before it came to the Tribunal? Once a case is heard in public, there will be a general sense of 'no smoke without fire'. Yet by settling out of court, the employers risk the stain of racism remaining on their own managers, who took the decision the consequence of which is being 'bought out'. Worst of all, how do you overcome the reluctance of those who may be entirely right-thinking but not particularly passionate about being fair to ethnic minority applicants, who may well feel that it is all too much trouble to make such an appointment in the first place?

I am clear that we cannot tackle these issues from outside. It is only if there are people closely involved in the process of recruitment and personnel management across a broad front that these issues can be confronted and overcome. Once again, engagement not withdrawal is the key. Those engaged, however, are unlikely to be dispassionate. If they are caught in the midst of unjust allegations, possibly against them personally, they will be affected and will value support. That support will be needed both on an individual issue and also for the broader principle of their continued involvement.

The example of unjust accusations of racial prejudice is just one of the many areas where engagement produces real problems and pressures. Fair treatment of women, harassment in the workplace, job redefinitions and redundancy, the minimum wage, all these and many more have made headlines while I have been drafting this chapter. For every instance, there are details which push sympathy and judgement one way or the other. Yet it is rare to find an example when we would conclude that the matter would have been better dealt with by someone without caring principles, and that the carer should leave these things alone for fear of being tainted by the inevitable pragmatism of most solutions. We need Quakers involved in coping with this type of management issue, even though wrestling with it will quite possibly do them personal harm, so that they can witness to our beliefs through the example they set. Therefore our Religious Society needs to offer those so involved our support, preferably through a partnership between those engaged and those who can offer the perspective, principle and support of being outside the 'commercial state' but not hostile to it.

Wealth-creation

At the heart of the modern Quaker's suspicion of business has been a growing discomfort with the concept of wealth-creation in the ordinary sense of the phrase. The view of the Quaker dynasties of the eighteenth and nineteenth centuries had been almost to venerate the individual's ability to build a successful commercial enterprise, provided this was done in accord with what we might call due commercial process. Writing in 1859, John Stephenson Rowntree complained that among Quakers then 'it had become commonly accepted that worldly achievements commanded the most respect. Though the meek might inherit the earth, it was the materially successful who had come to dominate.'[9]

Through the eighteenth and nineteenth centuries, running successful businesses (and as a consequence acquiring wealth and providing employment) were admired activities for Quakers, and high standards of commercial achievements were set and policed by Meetings. It has been suggested to me, persuasively, that Quaker involvement in industry and commerce came initially from the notion that all our gifts and talents are held in trust from God, and that we therefore have an obligation to develop them to their fullest potential. As well as ridding commerce of any supposed 'taint' as a consequence, the resulting success had direct benefits for the Religious Society, given concrete form (or stone) in the Friends Meeting Houses in London and Manchester. However, bankruptcy and business failure were so serious as to lead to investigation by fellow Quakers and very likely to disownment from membership. In August 1770 John Gurney and Robert Seaman inquired on behalf of Norwich Meeting into the insolvency of Thomas Neale 'which he acknowledges to be in Part owing to his Indiscretion; for which he expresseth himself deeply concerned'. The concern of the investigators was how to distance the Religious Society from such shortcomings: 'to clear our Society from the reproach brought thereon by his Misconduct, we can do no other than testify our Disunity with him, until he shall make such Satisfaction as becomes this meeting to receive'.[10]

In contrast, by the late twentieth century any conventional wealth had come to be regarded with at best circumspection, at worst with downright hostility. Some of this change of attitude can be traced to a growing awareness of the environmental costs of irresponsible wealth-production. Much of it, though, stems from what seems a rooted objection to wealth itself. David Shutt observes that 'most Quakers shut down when you come to talk about money'.[11] Yet we depend upon the creation of wealth to do what we want to achieve as a movement. Joseph Rowntree is said to have written the paper which gave birth to the Village Trust, the Social Service Trust and the Charitable Trust (the first two now the Rowntree Foundation and the Reform Trust respectively) between Christmas and New Year of 1904. Using perhaps half of his great fortune, these Trusts underpin much that is admirable in our society today.

The great commercial achievements of eighteenth and nineteenth century Quakers did not arise from regarding the accumulation of wealth as an end in itself. Stephen Overell, writing in the *Financial Times*, observed that 'the great irony of Quaker business is that they never wanted to be wealthy. George Fox...commanded his followers in 1652 to "beware the deceitfulness of riches". [Yet] in the eighteenth century Quakers dominated the list of families with more than £100,000 in wealth;...in the nineteenth century, Quakers exemplified the Victorian paternalists.'[12] Now we often seem ashamed of that part of our Quaker heritage (although not so ashamed as to refuse funds from their charitable trusts or to refuse to use the great Meeting Houses built with their fortunes). Indeed it might be argued that we have neglected our inheritance because of our suspicion at the way in which it was originally amassed, leaving the Religious Society much less well endowed in terms of capital than, say, the Methodist Church, which now deploys funds of around £1 billion.

Such prejudice is self-defeating. It is perhaps reasonable to base an argument for changing the way in which human endeavour is organised. For the present, however, without proper resource, wealth if you will, we are deprived of our ability to do much of what we wish. Ask those struggling to balance the books at Friends House, seeking to find the money to pay a fair wage in order to carry through the 'corporate work' which Yearly Meeting intends, and you will soon realise the implications of refusing to engage with this particular Angel. If we continue with our suspicion of wealth-creation, and of the creators of wealth, who will fund the future? Time and time again, when Friends cry 'what are we going to do about Nicaragua, or Mozambique, or Kosovo' we find we haven't the money. We are reaping already what our distrust of wealth has sown.

Ethical investment

A moving example of the dilemmas of wealth-creation can be found in the early years of the ethical investment movement, something with which Friends have been intimately concerned. Lyn Wilson's unpublished history of *The Stewardship Trusts and Friends Provident* is the story of 'how people may arrange their monthly savings, life assurance, personal pension or endowment mortgage through investments which do not invest freely in any quoted share or security but take account of ethical values.' Such investments are a most useful paradigm for responsible conduct of wealth-creation as a whole.[13]

Friends Provident as an institution originated in a concern led by Samuel Tuke and Joseph Rowntree in 1832. By 1975, the requirement for a majority of the board to be Quakers had been removed. Debates within Friends Provident in the 1980s culminated in a decision in June 1983 to abolish specific investment restraint for FP's investments as a whole, and this led two of the continuing Quaker directors to resign. It was due to the efforts of the two who remained, together with Richard Rowntree, that the first ethical investment fund to employ positive criteria was established in June 1984 as the Stewardship Trust. The idea was then 'sold' to City institutions to the point where it now represents by some margin the most substantial ethical fund in what is becoming quite a crowded market. (There are now fifty-five ethical funds, inspired at least in part by Stewardship's lead.)

These incidents, fresh enough still to be quite a painful memory for those involved, illustrate a classic dilemma of this book and lecture. When confronted in business (and, as the next chapter will discuss, in public life) with a circumstance which seems to clash with basic Quaker principles, should we stay engaged or withdraw? For the chairman of Friends Provident, Ted Phillips, the resignations made 1 June 1983 'one of the saddest days of my life'.[14] With the benefit of the hindsight of two decades, a fair conclusion might be that it was the *combination* of some

Friends staying engaged and some withdrawing which may have won the day. If we are unhappy with a turn of events, it is not enough simply to make a principled withdrawal. Some of us must stay and press for a positive outcome. Both groups are equally deserving of our support, if we are to forge a partnership which can renew Quaker relevance to these issues. The issue of demutualisation presents similar challenges today.

One of the most intriguing aspects of the Stewardship achievement is that it confronts the dilemma of how we can stay engaged with the commercial world in positive as well as negative terms. Too often the temptation in considering ethical investment (as it is in engaging with commerce as a whole from a principled standpoint) is to identify what we are against. More difficult, but at least as important, is to decide what we support, because in that way we can witness in the world to the benefit of society as a whole. Striving for positive outcomes, at least with those companies not irrevocably committed to unacceptable products and services, is going to be more effective in the long run than the external pressure which comes through 'activism' alone. Not for nothing is this approach to ethical investment known as 'responsible engagement'.

Investment criteria

It is instructive to look at the investment criteria adopted by the Stewardship Fund. These begin with positive activities by a company, which make a worthwhile contribution to society. They include: supplying the basic necessities of life; providing high quality products and services which are of long term benefit to the community; conservation of energy or natural resources; environmental improvements and pollution control; good relations with customers and suppliers; good employment practices; training and education; strong community involvement; a good equal opportunities record; and openness about company activities.[15]

This list is a fascinating statement of those aspects of modern enterprise which contribute positively to the way we live, here and overseas. It is also evidence of how engagement with the commercial process of financial investment, surely the area viewed by many Friends with the greatest suspicion, can be a practical force for good. To revisit my metaphor, it shows the types of blessings which can flow from wrestling with the Angel of investment.

It needs of course to be counterbalanced by a policy to avoid negative indicators, identifying activities which harm the world or its inhabitants. The negative list cites: environmental damage and pollution; unnecessary exploitation of animals; trade with or operations in oppressive regimes; exploitation of Third World countries; manufacture and sale of weapons; nuclear power; tobacco or alcohol production; gambling; pornography; and offensive or misleading advertising. Already I sense challenge and disagreement. The negative list is instantly more debatable, and that is even before you come to consider whether investment should entirely avoid a company which has any dealings at all with any of these activities. How much of a company's trade may be in one of these areas for it to be disallowed? Any at all? Under such-and-such a percentage? What if a company scores high on the positive factors, but poorly on one or more of the negative ones?

It is inescapable that ethical investment embodies compromise. It involves putting together a credible portfolio, which will perform adequately, but which does not compromise people's deeply held beliefs. There can be no perfect companies. Thus, there may be a perfectly good supermarket chain, providing service to local rural communities, with good environmental and employment policies, praiseworthy corporate governance, which retails tobacco. On the other hand, the growth of ethical investment is one of the most heartening features of the current commercial environment. There is evidence from the US to show that one in every eight dollars is invested under what is known as an 'SRI mandate', that is to say 'socially responsible investment'.[16] In the UK, a seemingly minor change in pension law, which took effect in June 2000, means that pension funds now have to tell their members whether they take into account other than financial factors when choosing investments. This is already leading to a quiet revolution as the SRI pension funds start to make real inroads. More than that, companies keen to keep pension fund investors will pay increasing attention to their environmental performance, for example, thus using a simple financial mechanism to effect real change in the level of social responsibility of industry as a whole.[17]

I believe the key here is that Quakers should not shy away from making such judgements. To do so, we need individuals who remain involved with the process in order to be in a position to influence these decisions, to 'tangle with reality'[18] in John Whitney's telling phrase. While some among us feel they must stand apart from participation in even such well-intentioned wealth-creation, for as long as our society remains its imperfect, commercial self, others must remain within the process to influence it for good. We also need to ensure that the business practices of the Religious Society measure up to best practice.

The ethical investment sector also illustrates how staying engaged can further the causes we support. Some such funds in the UK are now adopting the practice, common in the USA, of 'constructive dialogue' with companies. This may properly be seen as a form of direct action, of bearing witness against the wrongdoings of commerce, but from within the board room and with real power. Using in-house research, engaged ethical funds undertake active discussion and debate with the companies in which they invest in order to boost positive features and to get the companies to improve negative ones. Clearly, there is a judgement to be made whether the ethical cause can be better advanced by remaining as an investor, and using that lever to achieve change; or whether investment is unacceptable *per se*. We need people of principle and goodwill to be part of that decision-making process. Best of all would be a partnership in which those 'inside' and those 'outside' shared the same principles.

For the dilemmas do not stop there. One leading Independent Financial Adviser asks all their clients about their attitudes to investment risk and their ethical concerns.[19] 'Sometimes the results are contradictory... an individual who wants a long-term low-risk investment but has extremely strict ethical criteria may have to compromise on some of the investment possibilities.' This is a dilemma for Quaker enterprises as well. Staff at Friends House have to choose whether or not to select the 'unitised ethical option' for their pension investment. Those investing of our own Society funds must decide for example what level of environmental guarantees they seek, perhaps expressed as 'shades of green'. Are they satisfied to be merely 'light green', or do they wish to be 'medium green' or even 'dark green'?[20]

Then there is the matter of consistency. Do ethical standards change, or does the commercial world in which they are to be applied change? In practice, while the principles do not change, the ground on which they are applied is moving steadily all the time. One of the central dilemmas for the individual who wrestles with the Angel of commerce is that of moral relativism, so much harder to deal with than the absolutes.

Notes to Chapter 3

1 Margaret Forster *Rich Desserts and Captain's Thin* Vintage 1997 p 118
2 Ibid. p 120
3 James Walvin *The Quakers, Money & Morals* John Murray 1997 p 163
4 Ibid. p 210
5 Jonathan Dale *Beyond the Spirit of the Age* 1996 p 64
6 Ibid. p 54

7   Ibid. p 96

8   *The Spectator* 26 February 2000 pp 14–15

9   John Stephenson Rowntree *Quakerism Past and Present* 1859, summarised in Arthur Raistrick *Quakers in Science and Industry* Sessions Book Trust, York 1950 p 132

10 L S Pressnell *Country Banking in the Industrial Revolution* Oxford 1956 p 243 quoted in Walvin op. cit. p 73

11 Lord Shutt of Greetland in conversation with Tony Stoller 29.11.00

12 *Financial Times* 22 August 2000

13 Although Lyn Wilson's history is unpublished, there is a copy in the Library of Friends House

14 quoted in Wilson op. cit.

15 www.friendsprovident.co.uk/stewardship/policy

16 Social Investment Forum, Washington D.C. 4 November 1999

17 Roger Cowe 'Start of quiet revolution in pension funds' *Guardian* 30 June 2000

18 John Whitney in conversation with Tony Stoller 12 August 1999

19 *The Millennium Guide to Ethical & Environmental Investment* Holden Meehan 1999

20 Holden Meehan, ibid. asked their clients about their ethical concerns. 'Sometimes the results are contradictory. For example, an individual who wants long-term low risk investment but has extremely strict ethical criteria may have to compromise on some of the investment possibilities. As the market develops, however, the choice becomes less one of moral relativity (*sic*) and more one of identifying "decent" companies which stand to prosper in an economy where social responsibility plays an important part ... There is a correlation between risk and volatility, and the tightness of ethical criteria applied. In a nutshell the categories are: light green; medium green; dark green.'

4 Breaking the chains

Public administration and the state

There is no greater perversion of the ordered, documented process of government, than the Wannsee Conference. The banality of its setting increases the chill. Take the S-Bahn to Wannsee station on the outskirts of Berlin, and then bus 114 to the type of house where bureaucrats still gather to talk through tricky practical problems of administration. On the agenda for 20 January 1942 were questions such as how a Jew was to be defined, and awkward logistical issues of evicting, transporting, receiving and putting to death an entire race. As is normal practice for minutes concerned with process, a memorandum was circulated in advance to those attending. In an 'official, businesslike and objective way' it deals with the size of the problem: 'Around 11 million Jews come into consideration for this final solution of the Jewish question, who are distributed among the individual countries as follows: [among those listed were the 330,000 Jews in England and the 4,000 in Ireland]. In the process of carrying out the final solution, Europe will be combed through from west to east.' The minutes of the conference were written by Adolf Eichmann.[1]

Agenda; memoranda; minutes! Never can the obscenity of corrupt power have been so deployed through the routine techniques of governance in a modern, western state. That conference may have been inspired by evil maniacs, but the detail must have been carried through by secretaries, stenographers, administrators, typists, messengers and drivers effectively doing their normal, day-to-day jobs. These were the so-called *Schreibtischmörderer* (desk murderers). Wannsee stands as a permanent justification for all those who feel inspired to oppose the power of a corrupt state.

And yet, that is not the only lesson. This was as nightmarish a circumstance as anyone could ever fear to encounter, and my own Jewish heritage makes it difficult to consider objectively. Nevertheless the reality of the Wannsee Conference throws into stark relief the question of engagement in state affairs. If people of good will like Quakers reject participation in the heart of the state machine, then things will be done which we will find unacceptable; in certain extreme cases, horrifying. Yet if we want at least some among us to stay as part of the process, then we have to offer those who choose to wrestle with these matters a level of support to help them cope with the compromises forced upon them by their place in the system. As Jacob with the Angel, so these people will be damaged by their encounter.

My hope is that such people can form a partnership with others who are working outside the state. For them also circumstances can be horribly difficult. In 1938, Rufus Jones, George Walton and Robert Yarnall actually held a short Meeting for Worship in Gestapo Headquarters in Berlin, while seeking to negotiate some of the last Jewish evacuations. In all, the Quaker Berlin Centre may have achieved 1,135 emigrations.[2] Yet why had the outstanding work of Quakers in Germany in the Thirties so little impact on the broader policies? Possibly because there was no one within the system at a much earlier stage, when the full horror might have been averted, with whom they could forge a partnership to counter the evil alliance that was taking over. Friends had been obliged to conclude by September 1935 that 'unless the relief work was conducted very quietly in the future, British Friends would probably be asked to withdraw from Germany, individual German Friends might be arrested and the continued existence of German

Friends as a body would be imperilled.'[3]

John Bright and the Alexandria bombardment

John Bright's resignation from Gladstone's cabinet in 1882 further illustrates the dilemma. One of the beacons of Victorian Quakerism, and indeed one of the pillars of Liberal England, John Bright was a member of Rochdale Meeting, as his mill-owning father had been before him. He entered Parliament in 1843 as MP for Durham and joined Gladstone's first Cabinet in 1868, at the age of 57. In the late spring of 1882, Arabi Pasha, an Egyptian nationalist leader, had seized control of the government from the nominal Ottoman ruler, the Khedive. His biographer Keith Robbins notes that in May, as the British fleet took up station off Alexandria, Bright was not unduly disturbed. 'Time and patience, he believed, might solve the problem.'[4] It did not. On 11 July the fleet bombarded Egyptian forts at Alexandria, and Bright drafted three letters of resignation without sending any of them. A meeting with Gladstone the following day failed to persuade him and on 15 July he resigned.

Yet curiously, Bright did not try to mobilise opposition within the Cabinet, let alone more widely, to reverse the policy of armed response to this diplomatic problem. The short public statement which accompanied his resignation was considered by Gladstone's entourage to be 'in the best possible taste', an understatement given that if Bright had criticised the administration in public he might well have brought down the government.[5] I surmise that Bright found himself in the classic position of those who walk away, on a matter of principle, from that which they hold most dear. He had been a parliamentarian and a cabinet minister for much of his later years. At this moment of disengagement, his renowned zeal deserted him. He wrote to his daughter, Helen, in September, that 'I feel as if I was ready to resign everything & to run away...if I were not so desolate and lonely in the world I should do so.'[6] Like all of us, Bright's occupation, and his sense of being at the centre of affairs, fed many needs.

To stay or to go, to soldier on or to resign on matters of principle, when government or public affairs take a turn for the worse; what is a Quaker to do in such circumstances? Nothing in the Liberals' conduct of foreign affairs in the succeeding thirty years suggests that they, the nation or the world were better off for the absence of Bright's ability to influence the Prime Minister; nor do Bright's own diaries suggest he was any the happier for going. There is a strong case for keeping hold of the Angel for as long as we can.

Secrecy and freedom of information

One of the greatest practical difficulties facing Friends who are part of the political/administrative process is the system's natural tendency towards secrecy. Robin Robison has written of his growing disgust with the culture of secrecy he perceived in the Civil Service, and especially in the Intelligence Services.[7] This was, he says, a key factor in his resignation from public administration, and he quotes Peter Hennessy's view that 'secrecy is the bonding material which holds the rambling structure of central government together'.[8] Much of the work of the Committee for Truth and Integrity in Public Affairs, between 1991 and 1995, focussed upon the question of secrecy in government and the prospects for freedom of information. This is a good example of the issues facing Quakers who choose to remain engaged with the public affairs aspect of the 'commercial state'.

As chief executive of a statutory corporation, the Radio Authority, I continue to wrestle personally with issues in this broad area of secrecy: freedom of information, and its obverse, protection of privacy; and the role of whistleblowing. These serve to illustrate real and current dilemmas for at least one Quaker currently engaged at the point where business and public administration intersect.

Most public bodies suffer accusations of undue secrecy. That will inevitably arise from those who feel aggrieved in one way or another at the actions or decisions of those bodies. It is an easy accusation to make, and something which a vexatious complainant often alleges. It is not always true, but it is accurate often enough. In my own case, I know that there are significant areas of policy-making where we have not made public either the background information informing a decision or the reasons for that decision. I also know that this is not an evil perpetrated by a 'secret state', but the result of a genuine dilemma.

The Radio Authority awards commercial radio licences. These are valuable properties, worth millions of pounds, which are usually fiercely competed for. The criteria by which awards are made are set down in an Act of Parliament which is relatively uncontroversial in itself. However, the process of analysis conducted by the professional staff of the Authority of applications received was for many years kept secret as a matter of deliberate policy. There was a genuine concern that, if details of the process of analysis were revealed, instead of putting forward proposals for the best approach to providing a radio station in a locality, applicants would instead simply seek to match whatever system of marking and analysis was being used by the assessors. Similarly, for a long time no reasons were given for the final decision of the Authority, for fear of generating 'cloned' applications in the future. As a result of considerable heart-searching and challenging of conventional advice, both these policies were reversed. The outcome has been heartening. The process is now validly seen to be better and fairer. By exposing the system of analysis, and requiring the lay Members of the Authority to focus in their discussion on criteria which will be published, we are now more confident in our processes.

However, the matter does not stop there, nor do the dilemmas go away. Freeing the supply of information is not unlike peeling the layers off an onion. We are now being encouraged to make public our reasons for rejecting unsuccessful applicants, not just why we chose the winner. This raises several issues. As is the case when there are several competent applicants for one job, in the end the interviewing panel is charged with making a value judgement as to which will be the best suited, once the objective criteria have been applied. Furthermore, in making a positive choice, the Authority will not exhaustively assess the demerits of those rejected. To set out their failings in public (and invite consequent legal challenge) will require a much fuller analysis, and will make the process much more unwieldy and expensive. Is this a legitimate factor to take into account?

I believe it is. Efficient administration, which has adequate checks and balances to ensure fairness and accountability, is the proper goal. Openness and disclosure should be seen as a means to this end, not as an end in itself. Even if such fuller disclosure could be made, in many cases it would reveal little. I always keep in mind Gillian Reynolds' observation that 'whenever I hear the word "transparency" it makes me want to count the spoons'. There is no sacrament in openness, only a good practical Quaker wish for plain dealing and the speaking of truth.

There would be a further difficulty in making public the losers' reasons, and that brings us into the area of privacy. At times the Authority receives applications which are frankly bad. Perhaps well-intentioned individuals have put together a document which hugely misses the mark, or perhaps major operators in the business, who ought to know better, have fallen below the standards to be expected of them. In either of these cases, there would be distress caused to individuals by disclosure. On the one hand, you might very well argue that by applying for a public licence, applicants should accept possible criticism in public. On the other, I imagine Quakers generally might share the Authority's reluctance to exact such a price. Then again, arguably the Authority would be helping by setting out the failings, thus coaching applicants how to do better. It has been suggested that this could be done privately (secretly?) so that no public humiliation would result. Even assuming that such matters could or should remain confidential in our prurient times, would it be fair to coach only poor applicants, or indeed only failed previous applicants, ahead of further licence advertisement?

I have clear evidence that improved openness can be a gain all round. Yet we also continue to wrestle with the implications of full disclosure on process and privacy. The European Convention on Human Rights institutionalises this dichotomy. Article 10 preserves the right to freedom of expression, 'without interference by public authority'. Article 8 provides that 'everyone has the right to respect for his private and family life'. Reconciling these two rights, when for example a newspaper wishes to expose matters that would tarnish the reputation of a public figure, and call into question his or her fitness to hold office, will be simply another manifestation of this dilemma. We need people of good will engaged in its resolution, not excluding Quakers.

Whistleblowing

The concept of 'whistleblowing', as something more than simply pointing out error or abuse, has been developed as a direct counterbalance to unfair treatment of those who might have hoped that the frank pointing out of mistakes would serve both them and their organisations. There are far too many well-documented instances of unacceptable victimisation of those who have identified problems. I have chosen to deal with it here, in consideration of the state rather than of business practice, since it seems that it is in connection with public matters and the accountability of public bodies that the dilemmas are most clearly seen. Organisations such as Public Concern at Work have sought 'to promote compliance with the law and good practice in the public, private and voluntary sectors...[and to]...focus on the responsibility of workers to raise concerns about malpractice and the responsibility of those in charge to investigate and remedy such issues.' [9] The dual responsibility here is interesting and accurate; it is the task of employers to ensure that a whistle can be blown (and not to keep covert control by making it difficult) and equally of employees to make known their concerns fairly and robustly.

Thanks not least to the efforts of PCAW, the Public Interest Disclosure Act came into force in July 1999. It encourages people to raise concerns and requires employers including the state to make provision for this. So, provided there are clear and proper procedures in place, and individuals are prepared to take responsibility to use them, that's all sorted out then? Well, not quite. For both employee and employer there remain challenging dilemmas.

It is no light matter to decide to become a whistleblower. This is not the same as having a good moan, an enjoyable and necessary part of any work experience, or even the same as making a complaint. It is a decision to invoke formally a procedure which says that those for whom and/or among whom I am working are behaving improperly. Personal safeguards most certainly should be in place to prevent victimisation. In my own organisation, confidentiality is assured to those invoking this process, and a powerful external recipient is available for anyone who does not have confidence to raise a matter with the management or board; no less than the Departmental Permanent Secretary. Even so, we would all have to acknowledge the courage of someone who chose to attack their colleagues, and in a less scrupulous organisation very probably risk their livelihoods.

If we ever find ourselves challenged to blow the whistle, we would also, I think, want to test the validity of our concerns and the appropriateness of taking this route to deal with them. As Roland Carn writes in his assessment of the role of Quakers in Business and Quaker Enterprises, [10] 'truth does not always need to be spoken, but what is spoken does need to be true...Saying something just because you need to say it is an abuse. Telling the truth as you see it in a way that is misunderstood by your audience or in a way that is unnecessarily hurtful is an abuse.' The wish to whistleblow will, in each and every instance, raise for the individual a personal and moral dilemma that will need to be tested before the action is either taken or avoided. For Friends who might be in this position, we need to look to our Quaker mechanisms for Clearness, both to see whether they are in place and widely understood and to find out whether they are used.

For the employer, it is also necessary to create a culture where criticism is actively encouraged, and ideally where matters can be raised long before they get to the whistleblowing stage. Early in the life of the John Lewis Partnership, its founder John Spedan Lewis set up Committees for Communication in each of the JLP 'branches', the department stores, individual business and manufacturing units within the Partnership.[11] These comprised members of staff, excluding managers and supervisors, elected by their workmates in a secret ballot. They met and still meet regularly under an independent chairman, from outside the branch, who is himself accountable directly to the Chairman of the Partnership through a senior director who has overall responsibility for the operation of the Committees.

Members of the Committee discuss any points which they wish to make about the conduct of their part of the business. Once these are drawn out, the Managing Director of the branch is summoned to the meeting and, to avoid any risk of victimisation of individuals, the questions, complaints or suggestions are put to him by the independent chairman. An answer is mandatory, either then and there or after due research, and the proceedings of the Committee are published to all those working in the branch. As a system for preventing small items becoming large and damaging issues, for raising real abuses, and for building confidence between managers and staff in a huge organisation, it has yet to be bettered. To set it up, and to maintain it, required a willingness by those who initially owned and subsequently manage the business to expose themselves to challenge, to build a culture where the raising of problems is considered to be of benefit to the company or organisation.

One unspoken advantage of the John Lewis system is that it is less open to abuse by those who are not well-intentioned. For most organisations, though, embracing the concept of whistleblowing introduces the dilemma of how to deal with those who use it either deliberately to make mischief, or through misapprehension or inadequacy to the same effect. As I will discuss in more detail in chapter 6, the nature of our media-dominated society leaves even the best intentioned organisations and individuals very exposed to false accusation. While there are very properly safeguards for the employee, the unscrupulous or obsessed person can readily use whistleblowing, the courts or the press to bear false witness. Much of our media take delight in spoiling reputations by reporting such accusations. Once an organisation is known to have had the whistle blown against it, irrespective of the rights and wrongs of the case (which are often hardly reported at all) the 'no smoke without fire' syndrome emerges once again, and it risks permanent harm.

Jubilee 2000 and Transport 2000

There exists now a new approach to politics, building new alliances and working within the state, deploying the techniques of the system and some carefully applied direct action. The growth of legal activism, aimed at bringing about social change, has been a notable element in the work done towards freedom of information and the current introduction of Human Rights legislation. That is likely to be a dominant theme for the next few years at least. It has become clear that what I refer to as a 'partnership' approach can achieve real and lasting change in public policies. This is a major potential growth point for Quakers and the causes we support, if we can build the bridges needed between our aspirations and the 'commercial state'. Further, there is increasing evidence that direct action on its own, or in a campaign where it is dominant, is much less effective than an alliance between the activists and the insiders. Two key policy areas show the potential for success with the new politics; another, the continuing failure of the old way.

Andrew Marr writes a fascinating summary of the reversal of public policy towards road-building achieved in the early 1990s by the Transport 2000 coalition, originally founded by environmentalists and railway unions in 1973 as a counterbalance to the runaway successes of the British Road Federation.[12] 'A variety of tactics ... are used to push the case against more road-building. One Whitehall mandarin reckoned that the environmentalists were working cleverly at several levels: first the "nice cops" like the RSPB and the CPRE, speaking in polite, well-modulated tones, were trying to persuade ministers and policy-making officials, using detailed arguments and the unspoken electoral threat of their big memberships. They were extremely well-informed about the latest scientific data, sometimes more so than Whitehall itself. Then there were the direct-action "nasty cops" and the organisers of demonstrations, pickets and letter-writing campaigns.'

As the coalition gathered strength, some environmental groups began to regard the DoE as 'their' department and to promote its interests. Ministers, in turn, began to find that the more 'establishment' lobbyists in the green movement were 'people they could do business with', inside the system rather than outside. Marr notes that the role of Conservative MPs became increasingly important, since many of the direct-action protesters were supported by local residents and by Conservative voters. The change in the climate of official opinion was noticed even by the British Road Federation, which withdrew its support for the controversial and pivotal Oxleas Wood road scheme. Government withdrawal followed. A year later in 1995 'the new Transport Secretary Brian Mawhinney announced that, in effect, Britain had enough roads and that future spending would concentrate more on improving and repairing current ones, rather than building more. Something momentous had happened in British politics.'[13]

In the shifting pattern of politics, causes are rarely conclusively won or conclusively lost, and the roads issue remains. Marr's point

47

is best seen as showing, accurately, that new alliances, working within an increasingly receptive system, can achieve huge policy shifts, and that this represents genuinely new politics. I take that further to stress that these achievements are won by the new politics of engagement precisely in those areas where the old politics of withdrawal and external protest have achieved so little on their own.

The Jubilee 2000 coalition is dedicated to persuading the rich Western nations to cancel the unpayable debt owed by the world's poorest countries, under a fair and transparent process. As I write towards the end of 2000, there have been significant successes but not yet a final crowning conclusion. The Group of Seven (G7) leaders claimed, after their meeting in Cologne in June 1999, to have written off up to $100 billion of debt owed by the world's most impoverished nations. Vying to gain the approval of the coalition (a remarkable and revealing circumstance in itself) the British Chancellor and the American President have swapped public commitments to go further. On 6 November 2000, President Clinton signed legislation that provided $435 million in debt relief for heavily indebted poor countries.[14] As I type the final draft of this book, the UK Government has announced on 2 December 2000 that it is writing off the debts of the twenty poorest nations. The response of the world community to the Mozambique flood disaster was not only to send aid and logistical support, but also to suspend the requirement of that afflicted country to continue its debt repayments.

Jubilee 2000's 'debt-cutters' handbook, *Breaking the Chains*,[15] lists among its patrons mainline politicians, establishment clerics and leading academics. Its institutional members read like a roll-call of the caring great and good, from ActionAid to the YWCA. It deploys an equivalent range of methods to Transport 2000, working within the political system through direct involvement with the UK Treasury and parallel government departments overseas; and using modern techniques to support its direct action which included running a radio station as part of an international conference in Birmingham in 1996.

It seems harsh to draw a contrast between the relative successes of Transport 2000 and Jubilee 2000 and the relative failures of direct action for peace and particularly nuclear disarmament, not least as these things are properly assessed over decades not years. Nevertheless, since the high days of the early Aldermaston marches the old peace protest politics have little to show in real terms for the level of commitment which has been put into them, largely because they have lost their constituency within government. Even when the perceived strategic need among the super-powers for excessive nuclear arsenals has all but vanished, those arsenals remained long after the need had evidently ended, partly because the politics of protest made it almost impossible for governments to retreat from maintaining them. Work is now needed within the system to point out the very practical reasons for nuclear disarmament, not just at the gates of Greenham and Faslane.

The very open questions raised by the new US government's wish to include Fylingdales in their 'star wars' nuclear shield offer a real opportunity to make a difference to policy decisions by more than just direct action. As I write, this is an issue where the UK Government is not clear what to do, and informed advice could well persuade it to at least an approximation of virtue. Yet there are so few Quakers in positions where they can bring the pressure of reasoned argument and knowledgeable advice to bear from within government, parliament and administration in the way that the anti-roads and anti-debt campaigners have done. The work of the Oxford Research Group (see page 65) is an example of what can be achieved in the type of inclusive partnership between activists and engaged individuals. That feels to be the way forward for effective peace work in the new century, and it represents the new politics of engagement, of wrestling with the Angel at close quarters.

One further example of new politics may serve to illustrate the effectiveness of new methods. In 1993 the BBC proposed to move

Radio 4 from long wave, arguing (with some justification) that this was now an anachronism. An alliance was formed called 'Save Radio Four' which worked at the highest levels of government and public life, through the press and by personal contact, to reverse the decision. It was successful, and Radio 4 long wave is on air to this day. The campaign combined pulling the levers of power within the 'commercial state' with a unique version of that staple of direct action, the protest march. As the police accompanying the procession decided that their main task was to stop grey-haired ladies and frail donnish men from falling under the wheels of passing buses, rather than safeguarding public order, the marchers' chant swelled up:

> 'What do we want? – Radio Four!
> 'Where do we want it? – Long Wave!
> 'What do we say? – Please!'

Sometimes the new politics is irresistible.

Notes to Chapter 4

1 Noakes and Pridham (eds.) *Nazism vol. III*, no. 850 quoted in Alan Bullock *Hitler and Stalin* HarperCollins 1991 p 843
2 Hans A Schmitt *Quakers and Nazis: Inner Light in Outer Darkness* Missouri University Press 1997 pp 108–9
3 *Friends Committee for Refugees and Aliens* 1933–1950 Lawrence Darton p 13
4 Keith Robbins *John Bright* Routledge & Kegan Paul p 245
5 Robbins op. cit. p 246
6 Ibid.
7 Two essays by Robin Robison in *Questions of Integrity* London Yearly Meeting 1993; see pp 6–12 and 21–35
8 Peter Hennessy *Whitehall* Fontana Press 1990 p 346 quoted in Robison op. cit. p 21.

9 www.pcaw.demon.co.uk

10 Roland Carn *Towards a Quaker View of Business* (Quakers in Business Group 1 November 1999). The resulting publication *Good Business: Ethics at Work* is now available.

11 *The Gazette*, the weekly magazine of the John Lewis Partnership, describes the organisation as follows:

'The Partnership is a retail business run on co-operative principles ... The Business belongs to those who work in it. All except those engaged temporarily are Partners from the day they join, and all the ordinary share capital is held by a trustee on their behalf.

Under irrevocable trusts Partners get all the profits, after provision for prudent reserves ... The Partnership aims to run its business efficiently and competitively, and at the same time to enable its members to enjoy full information about it, to express their views freely, to co-operate in shaping its policies, and to share in its rewards. Management is accountable to the general body of Partners, in particular through elected councils and through the Partnership's journalism.'

12 Marr op. cit. pp 311ff.

13 Ibid. p 314

14 *Economist* 18.11.00 p 141

15 *Breaking the Chains* Jubilee 2000 Coalition, 1999

5   Quaker plc

Effective conduct of Quaker enterprises

The lecture which provides the occasion for this book is to be given at Yearly Meeting, the main business Meeting of the Religious Society of Friends in the UK. Here you will see Quakers doing their own version of networking; even, indeed, you will see them 'working' the room or courtyard between formal sessions. That immediately points up a paradox. In this most spiritual of weeks, the weightiest of Friends can be observed doing the sorts of things which delegates at highly secular conferences do. Yearly Meetings have times of great spirituality. Nevertheless, here religious values and temporal habits most clearly collide. You are suddenly aware of being part of an undertaking, not just a religious movement, which has budgets, staffing establishments, property portfolios and much of the rest of the apparatus of an enterprise of the 'commercial state'.

In the previous chapters I have argued that Quakers – or some of us at least – need to engage with the 'commercial state', in business, public administration and media. Yet from the experience of Yearly Meeting we also are inescapably given to understand that the secular will intersect with our enterprises whether we wish it or not. In this chapter, therefore, I will examine how our own Quaker structures and enterprises (in a non-commercial sense) are affected by the 'commercial state', and what lessons we might learn. The next chapter will look at how we put our Quaker case to the wider world, and chapter 7 considers how an individual Quaker might therefore respond. Clearly, these three sets of issues are intertwined. More than that, even individuals who believe they are safely outside the 'commercial state' will find themselves engaging with the commercial or administrative worlds as an unintended consequence of the society in which we live; as customers, as voters, as patients, as employees.

The business of Quakerism
Our Religious Society is a business. We own a prime piece of real-estate on London's Euston Road in the form of Friends House, and Meeting Houses and other properties across the UK. We are employers of over a hundred staff in our central, 'corporate work', and are therefore providers also of salaries, pensions and benefits. We employ numbers of people as wardens and field-workers up and down the country and overseas, and many more on shorter-term bases, for instance to run projects and undertake specific tasks such as research or teaching. To do all this we must raise funds, place and sustain investments, and we have to manage the business. We therefore have first-hand experience of the dilemma facing any enterprise which wishes to be both effective and ethical.

The basis on which we wish enterprises to be conducted has been long established in our Quaker business traditions and does not change greatly, although the emphasis may shift from time to time. If we blend the traditional Quaker values for the conduct of a business enterprise, or for involvement in the state, with our more recent experience, we arrive at a set of familiar but challenging principles which I discuss in chapter 7. These demand the maintenance of a single standard of morality in all enterprises, whether commercial, public or private.

Historically, the translation of these principles into practice, and their supervision, was strict and the consequences of slippage

53

were harsh. There are frequent examples, from the beginning of the eighteenth century up to the end of the nineteenth, of disownment from membership because of bankruptcy. Raistrick[1] reports that John Kelsall, a leading Quaker active in the Darby iron concerns in the 1720s, could not bring himself to write the word 'bankruptcy', falling back on 'B_____'. The eventual sanction against bankruptcy was disownment from membership. It was common, indeed Walvin refers to the disownment of Elizabeth Fry's husband in 1828 as 'inevitable' despite the pain and humiliation it caused for an already renowned Quaker.[2]

Even allowing that the broader attitudes of society to bankruptcy have moderated, this seems strange to our modern way of thinking, at least in part because of the widespread unease in the Religious Society with commercial enterprise of any sort. It is almost as if failing in a commercial enterprise is better than succeeding in it (whilst not entering into it at all is best of all!). Our ecological radicalism has a tone of moral superiority about it which is at times pretty self-righteous. Yet, as we have seen, the Religious Society itself is 'in trade'. Further, since trade is going on it is better to have some Quakers involved leading by example in the nineteenth century fashion, than to leave the field.

In running 'Quaker plc' – Britain Yearly Meeting and our 'corporate work' – we need to settle our attitude to how the money we need is to be raised. Charity fundraising has certain established principles which many Friends find difficult. You can most easily get donations from those who have already given. Hence the use by other fundraisers of databases of givers or members to whom you then write personal letters soliciting donations. Charities and other ethical organisations know that eighty per cent of their income comes from twenty per cent of those giving. Thus we need to acknowledge without discomfort the extent to which we need to woo that higher stratum of givers. Anyone walking in a central London street will have encountered the teams from major national charities, with coloured tabards and clip boards, seeking support and donations. Yet what has become of the bucket collection at Yearly Meeting?

It is time we stopped being so precious on these matters, and became at the same time both more principled and more realistic. We need money for our 'corporate work', and a good deal more than the present system of unintrusive schedules can provide. Whilst we could of course reduce that 'corporate work' further to just such a level as pure funding will allow, that seems a negation of our witness. If we wish to continue with something like the present level of activity, as a minimum, then we have to use, appropriately, the techniques which everyone in our society is now accustomed to, but to do so in a way which is in line with our basic principles. There is nothing wrong in using a membership mailing list to tell Friends about what is done with their money, and what could be done with more. Nor is there anything wrong in a personal letter generated by such a system, so long as we ensure that those who do not want to receive such letters can easily say so without being made to feel in any way uncomfortable; surely a straightforward matter for our local collectors.

The eighteenth and nineteenth century Quaker networks trusted each other in financial matters, and accepted openness about who could and who could not afford to support their Meeting. Walvin writes that 'the ideals of Quaker life were not a simple mantra to be memorised and recited at particular moments. They were enforced by a structure of management which was more intrusive and manipulative than many have recognised, and was carried on throughout the nineteenth and into the twentieth century. To be a Friend necessarily involved subjecting oneself to possible scrutiny of one's personal and professional life.'[3] That goes too far for our modern judgements. But at the opposite extreme, in our introverted wish not to hurt feelings or to confront financial issues, we do our Meetings and our Friends a disservice, since the outcome is less 'corporate work' and less truth between ourselves.

Our instinctive unease with money makes us uncomfortable in dealing with it openly. That makes the Religious Society less accessible to those who have more than most and might be very willing for their wealth to witness through corporate action. Just as was the case with those Yearly Meeting buckets, there is a reluctance to accept that if we were more open with ourselves and each other regarding money, many of those who are able would welcome the generally joyous opportunity to give more.

We need to take the same approach to the way in which we husband and invest our funds. As I have discussed in chapter 4, there exists now a wide range of investments and financial institutions specifically designed to take account of ethical issues for investors. How are we to choose between them? Once again, we should work from our principles for corporate activity, seeking the best vehicles for achieving what our Quaker Business needs in any particular set of circumstances. This is not an issue which can simply be passed over to a small group of treasurers or whomever, to be done out of sight of the greater part of Friends. Decisions about how to use our wealth and how to protect our business should be taken by Friends together. It is central to how our enterprises run, and we all need to feel a sense of ownership in those decisions.

If that is to happen effectively, however, we need to help Friends to understand the investment issues available to them, the principles against which they can judge those opportunities, and help them to overcome their dislike or even fear of such matters. The more inclusive we are when wrestling with these matters, the more we can achieve prayerfully. To be informed, we need those among us who understand these issues from working with them, and are neither over-enamoured nor over-sceptical about them, and we need to involve such people in these decisions. We cannot turn our back on the best means to raise funds simply out of a misplaced delicacy towards money. We ought to establish the basic principles involved at the root of effective financial husbandry, identify how they can be translated to our own condition and be in line with our own tenets of proper conduct, and then choose the right technique for any particular circumstance.

Quaker Management Methods

Quakers ought to be today in the vanguard of good practice in managing our own enterprises and 'corporate work' just as once we were. That involves simple, open, skilled and principled management, not the adoption of short-lived fashions or unnecessary bureaucracy. We have among us plenty of people used to deploying good management techniques, but they often find themselves adrift and bewildered by what passes for best practice in the Religious Society. Quaker enterprises have generally little understanding of, and no natural affinity with, the reality of good management methods and business language.

The outcome is damaging. First, we spend a disproportionate amount of our time worrying about 'structures'. That would be regarded in the outside world as a sure sign of an organisation which had lost touch with its core functions and purpose. Second, we express those thoughts at times in a corrupted 'management-speak' which would have alarmed the Birtist reorganisers of the BBC in their heyday. As someone used to the layout and language of business papers, I not infrequently feel that Friends House papers are obscure. As I read of yet another set of papers about organisational restructuring, I feel that either I am missing something or that they are. Even the way we lay out documents with endless numbers, sub-numbers, and sub-sub-sub-numbers suggests that we are too often disguising the fact that these either have nothing to say or that we have no confidence in the clarity of thought they contain. Third, we allow adherence to what we wrongly perceive as good management practice to blind us to the essentials. By chance, I was sent as I was finishing this text a draft document from Friends House which is intended to be 'a popular version of the Five Year Plan' for distribution to all Members. It has seventy-six bullet points of either 'key [sic] principles', options, issues, missions or the like. Whatever did the 'unpopular' version look like?

This is not a wrong-turning exclusive to Friends. So many of our non-commercial institutions which are now being obliged to fall in with a 'management' approach – schools, colleges, hospitals – are in the same bind. They adopt the vocabulary without realising its limitations, and too often the more gross practices of the commercial world without realising that these are rejected by the vast majority of professional managers. The difference is that they are having corporate-speak and corporate-think forced upon them. We seem to have imposed it on ourselves. I am keen that we should indeed use the best techniques of the business world in conducting our own Quaker enterprises; but not the worst. That means less of the redundant business jargon, not more. Those whose working lives make them at home with the nature of organisational structure would ensure that form follows function, not the reverse. And they would recoil from the quantities of paper, which guarantee that no one can see the wood for the recycled trees.

In her 1994 Swarthmore Lecture, Margaret Heathfield wrote of the difficulty for our corporate structures in being a genuine repository for concerns, not least because of the difficulties of the interface with Meeting for Sufferings.[4] That worry has not diminished over the subsequent half dozen years. Part of the problem, which professional managers know well, is that structures as such do not provide solutions. At best, they help the people involved to work either collectively or individually to find and implement those solutions. Once the structures take over, however, any energetic and motivated operators will find ways of working outside them.

Again, we need to understand better what are the valuable methods of management, when and how to apply them, and when not to. If we have not built a partnership with those who are at home in the 'commercial state', then when we come to try and use its techniques we will do so at best only imperfectly. More than that, we need also to be able to judge when to trust our own business method over the imperfections of the secular systems. Many Friends have come to feel that Meeting for Sufferings has become the subject of 'steering' and 'management' from its Committee and from its table, as a substitute or even obstacle to the right holding of Meetings for Business. Writing in *The Friend*, David Bartlett observed that 'a body which is only allowed to hear good news cannot provide discernment of the depth Yearly Meeting deserves.'[5] This may be one reason for the increasing perception that Sufferings has lost much of its effective authority among British Friends. There may be a parallel here with the decline in the influence of Parliament in our national polity. But dissatisfaction with Sufferings also in part arises from a sense that the hierarchy of Friends within the Religious Society is hidden from all who are not natural participants in Friends House activities.[6]

Margaret Heathfield writes of her worry that the secular technique of a 'hidden agenda' infects our Business Meetings.[7] I think it is bound to do so, if we use inappropriately and without proper understanding the techniques of the 'commercial state'. If we had more intuitive appreciation of those (because we felt no hindrance in engaging with them, and we welcomed their exponents among us), then we would know better which fit our corporate principles; and which need to be firmly put aside when we meet to seek the leadings of the spirit in our business concerns.

One of the real difficulties we encounter is in getting genuine feedback from Friends at large about our corporate activity. Some of that is structural, with Monthly Meetings failing to involve just that section of our membership – those younger, busier, more currently engaged with commercial or administrative life – who we most need to input their understandings of the strengths and weaknesses of secular method. But we also fail to encourage that plain-speaking on which in theory we pride ourselves. Individually, we too often put being kind ahead of being truthful. At an institutional level, there is a tendency to wish to select what information is shared and how. For many years past, *The Friend* has felt constrained about writing a plain account of a scratchy Meeting for Sufferings, as we are used to see other, secular councils reported. Our journalists' perception that they might as a consequence lose their observer status at Sufferings is news management of which any government spin doctor would be proud. And I am in no doubt that *The Friend* is at times actively 'discouraged' from carrying material which the hierarchy finds inconvenient, just as happens to those writing reports on other aspects of our Quaker enterprises. Speaking truth to power, and plain speaking at that, is a principle to be embraced as much within the Religious Society, as by Quakers in society at large.

Bridging the divide

I have written about deploying 'commercial state' techniques in our own affairs, by seeking out the principles of good practice and applying them in rather different ways. We could take that a step further, and build it into a way of going about things which would benefit our Quaker enterprises and also offer a useful witness in the wider world.

A central error, not unique to Friends, is to mistake the outward forms of management practice for an underlying truth. For instance, the prevalence of short-term contracts in any established and permanent organisation would be regarded in the 'commercial state' as bad practice. It unsettles staff, diluting their commitment and exploiting their loyalty. Yet we do this to a surprising degree for Friends House staff, citing uncertainty of future funding. If we were to use the principles of good employment in the 'commercial state' properly, we might well wish to re-examine our present practice. If we did that, we should not focus on the principles of employment first, but on the funding problems which produce this poor practice.

That applies also in reverse. We have a great deal to offer to the 'commercial state', which can be of direct benefit to, for example, business success. The technique of staff appraisals has been imported into the caring professions from the 'commercial state' often in a crass and ineffective way. Why not take a lead to refine the process, by precept and example? Take our concept of God in every person and focus in the appraisal process on the strengths which each individual can offer, rather than their weaknesses. Here again, there is a basic principle which can be carried across the bridge between the two sectors. Similarly, the concept derived from our approach to the right holding of Meetings for Business, that the right decision need not always be either a majority view or even a consensus, offers a basis for a new approach to decision-making in certain circumstances. But non-Quaker enterprises need to know how this works, when it is appropriate and how the leadings of the spirit can be directly practical, rather than seeing only the outward forms and thinking them merely quaint and anachronistic.

This is another example of where we need to build a bridge between our Quaker approach and that of the 'commercial state', a bridge that can carry two-way traffic. The central idea, of looking behind the form to the essence of a technique, approach or principle, is a highly practical, moral notion which could be one of our significant contributions to modern life in the new century. We need Quakers engaged with and influential in the 'commercial state', to effect this transfer of ideas.

Notes to Chapter 5

1 Raistrick op. cit. p 116
2 Walvin op. cit. p 131
3 Ibid. p 208
4 *Being Together* Margaret Heathfield QHS 1994 pp 83–4
5 *The Friend* 2 February 2001 p 8
6 *The Friend* 2 February 2001 p 2; HJA's commentary notes that 'The table should be led by the body of the Meeting, not the other way round.'
7 Heathfield op. cit. p 93

6 Only smoke and mirrors?

Presenting the Quaker case

For our Quaker enterprises, as for those businesses and causes in which individual Quakers find themselves involved, it is impossible to engage with the world at large without considering the techniques for achieving publicity and wielding influence. What we do corporately requires coming to terms with how we make it public. It is one of the central failings of modern polity that presentation is thought to be separate from substance. You will hear often the cynical cry that what you say is less important than how you say it. That is wrong, but the two are intertwined in a way which many among us will find uncomfortable.

For example, our Peace Testimony has long been a matter on which we have sought to persuade governments and authorities to virtue. Skill in presenting it is of the greatest importance, for however good our message if it goes unheard it will not be acted upon. The famous *Declaration from the Harmless and Innocent People of God Called Quakers* addressed to Charles II, which is the text of our Peace Testimony, was a political as much as a religious document. Punshon notes that it was designed 'to disassociate the Quaker movement from the Fifth Monarchists'.[1] It was, in effect, a piece of lobbying, putting a 'spin' on the state perception of this movement.

The conclusion of the Declaration reads:

> This is given forth from the people called Quakers, to satisfy the king and his council, and all those who have any jealousy concerning us, that all accusations of suspicion may be taken away, and our innocency cleared.

And again, in a postscript:

> This is to clear our innocence from the aspersion cast upon us, that we are seditious or plotters.

George Fox, quoting this in his Journal, observes with evident relief that 'this declaration somewhat cleared the air'.[2]

We now have a range of issues, from the arms trade and child soldiers to the justice and penal systems, where we wish to bear witness to some effect. We want what we have to say to be heard and to have effect, because we believe that these are promptings from God to put right some of the hurts of the world.

The lobbyists and the lobbied

If we wish to be paid attention to then we need to use such techniques of the modern world as are consistent with our principles and our faith. I have written in chapter 4 of the successes of the new politics compared with the relative failure of 'pure' protest. It is clear that to achieve change in many of the areas which are of concern to us we need thorough research, a wide coalition of interests, access to the points of power and decision, and the ability to influence them. That means joining together in an approach which can enter the gates of policy-making to be heard there, as well as demonstrating a wide level of support outside the walls. That is not inconsistent with our principles. It only becomes so when we find ourselves asked to keep the company of groups who would act in a way we find unacceptable. In that circumstance we would not accept that any end can justify the means to be used. But short of such a position, we need to be open to the leadings of others, and the things that they can bring to a collective enterprise.

Those coalitions will want to use the modern techniques of political persuasion. So should we in our other, unique efforts. The plain speaking of truth to power means having something well thought through to say, and then seeking the opportunity to say it to the right people to good effect. One part of that will be achieved by giving proper scope to our Parliamentary Liaison; the other will be to harness Quakers who have such access. Yet too often we shrink back, because we feel uncomfortable with the process. Letter-writing we feel is fine, but letter-writing mostly has minimal effect. Our last Quaker MP, Richard Body, counsels that many of his colleagues are dismissive of 'Quakers from leafy suburbs with time and a typewriter'.[3] Of course we know that we aren't (all) like that, but if that is how we are perceived then that is the level at which we will have or not have effect.

We need to be active in the policy forums and in the think-tanks, and to encourage Friends so involved to use the Quaker virtues to good effect. That in turn means that we need the resources to prepare policy position papers and documents which can propound our case, and which can brief those whom we ask to make it. And it means that the Religious Society as a whole needs a ready mechanism to agree and endorse such positions. We must be prepared to cross the line into unfamiliar ground and wrestle with these issues in the policy forums, select committees, conferences and seminars where such decisions are made. If we take our plain speaking and our fair dealing, our tolerance and above all our example out and about, with people who are informed and speak with the prayerful support of Friends, we will be in a real position to influence the larger trends. In that way we can also enhance the witness of individual Friends and groups on specific local issues.

The Oxford Research Group was established in 1982 to carry out research into the structures and processes of nuclear weapon decision-making worldwide. It is an independent team of researchers and support staff whose policy is to make accurate information available on processes which its Annual Report points out are 'often obscure and undemocratic'. Funded by foundations, charities and individuals, many of which have Quaker links, it has no political affiliations, and notably it does not campaign.[4] It is an excellent example of how to use the new politics which I discussed in chapter 4, so long as it can link with those who have direct access to decision making.

Yet where among us are the people with access? As I write there remains just one Quaker Member of Parliament, Richard Body, who is to retire at what is at this date the 'next' General Election. The new Parliament is unlikely to have elected to it any further Quaker. The upper House has two Quaker life peers, Tom Taylor and David Shutt. This level of Parliamentary participation represents a huge pulling back from our traditional level of engagement. The origins of the Quaker Parliamentary Committee go back to November 1685. Michael Bartlett's researches show that there were ten Quaker MPs in 1885 (all Gladstone Liberals)[5] when the Religious Society was fully engaged in both the commercial and political worlds. The fine achievements of those lobbying through QUNO, for example in achieving genuine progress on the child soldiers issue, illustrates what might be achieved by so many more of us here at home, through quiet words in small circles. There is no substitute for being engaged in the centre of decision making.

Where there are Friends with the privilege of access, we are poor in using them. We also have no strategy for husbanding our diminished resources in this respect. Tom Taylor counsels that we need to choose to tackle only those public issues where we have something worth saying and where our involvement can make a real difference.[6] These will often be in areas where there is a Quaker tradition of action, since we need to acquire and demonstrate authority if we are to win respect for our representations. However, that presupposes a genuine will to have such influence, which our half-hearted support for involved Quakers must call into question. Harry Albright writing in *The Friend*[7] reported that

Meeting for Sufferings was 'polarised' on whether Friends should have anything to do with the upper chamber of Parliament. We are half-hearted indeed if we reject those who offer their engagement as part of any partnership for renewed Quaker effectiveness in public affairs.

Robin Robison[8] speculates that some of this new quietism [*my word here, not his*] arose at least in part from a reaction to the wartime efforts of Friends, which by 1945 had drained much energy, thus requiring a time of reflection and renewal. Nevertheless, even as late as 1945 there were nine Quakers in the Commons, and in 1983 there were at least thirteen standing as candidates for election to the Commons.[9] Many Friends are active in party politics, including distinguished service on local authorities, but Gerald Priestland's maxim holds good that a 'Church as a whole should be a rather bad party member ... its political function should be to haunt the politician, telling him what he would rather not hear'.[10] A number of Quakers participate in public administration and the Civil Service, but even so the clear impression overall is of a voice once heard loud and clear in debate and government now reduced to a quiet and occasional contribution.

Much of the work of our Committee for Truth and Integrity in Public Affairs (TIPA) is now focussed upon economic justice issues, seeking to ameliorate some of the effects of global markets and finance. If the Committee accurately reflects the consensus of Friends' wider concerns, as I believe it does, then engagement with UK politics does not feature high on our list nowadays. That may explain why there will soon be no Quaker MPs at all, despite the number of Friends working in higher education, which is these days such a fertile source of parliamentarians. Richard Body points out how much less room there is in party politics these days for convictions as distinct from ambitions.[11] Nevertheless, we must conclude that Quakers have become largely quietist in politics, to the great detriment of our ability to have our witness heard and respected. We have also failed to attract active sympathy from more than a handful of those non-Quakers who are so engaged. We are being derelict in our duty to make our witness effective.

Outside politics, we also have much that we wish the wider world to know about. That is for many reasons, although perhaps least of all to proselytise. We want our witness to attract support, so that it can be more effective. We want to test our ideas in the field, to check the validity of our concerns. We want to influence others to good, and to hearten them to have the courage to pursue their own concerns in their own way. In short, we wish to inform the wider world, in order to persuade it to virtue. Note that 'to inform in order to persuade' is the standard definition of commercial advertising.

We need to give to our Quaker enterprises the support of good and effective publicity and press coverage, not to feel that this is somehow unquakerly. The open air preachers and the pamphleteers of the seventeenth century had no such reluctance, nor should we. Where we should be testing our approach is not whether or not to do such things but how, and which of the possible techniques to reject. In that way we not only get necessary attention for our witness, we can also set the example that enterprises can conduct themselves effectively and persuasively in public without descending into unacceptable practices.

There will be a price to pay, as there is always some harm from wrestling with such a matter. That will include a measure of public scrutiny of who we are and what we do, and at times a searching test of what we profess. It will lead to unfair and at times hurtful criticism. Without this, though, our testimonies become irrelevant or at best merely monastic in their impact. Quakers in the past have not shied away from uncomfortable public confrontation. Many individuals among us do not do so today. Our Quaker enterprises should not do so either.

The spinners and the spun
The modern age is far too much in awe of the media. We have come to regard one journalist interviewing another journalist

about a topic designated by a third, the editor, as having genuine significance. The media find their highest wish-fulfilment when they seem to have become the message (although they complain bitterly if they suffer the fate of the messenger down the ages who brings bad news to rulers!)

I have spent two-thirds of my working life in print and broadcast media, as practitioner, manager, promoter and regulator. Although this book and this lecture are entirely my own (and none of the views here, particularly in this chapter, may be imputed to the Radio Authority which is my employer), my scepticism about the genuine significance of the media in their own right – rather than as a reflector of society – is shared by many of those in 'the business'. At times of reflection or of stress, you may hear colleagues say 'well, it's only smoke and mirrors'; or perhaps, in the commercial radio trade, 'it's only rock and roll'.

Nevertheless, the way society operates these days is conditioned by the channels of information and entertainment, which are what we really mean when we speak of 'the media'. If, as my thesis runs, we must not always shrink from engaging with society, then we must engage also with the media which affect it and reflect it. That raises two groups of questions. What is the current nature of the media themselves, and to what extent should we be working either to confirm or to change that; and how may Quaker enterprises seek to deal with the consequences of the symbiosis between the media and society.

Paradoxically, for all its presumed influence over the way we live and think, the trade of journalism is held in pretty low esteem. Journalists, doing their jobs properly, have never enjoyed the unalloyed approval of those in authority. It is the job of press and broadcasting to challenge, seek out and expose impropriety, to question current assumptions and to deflate the self-important. However, present disquiet extends so far because of three current characteristics, which we see displayed all too often: wanton disregard for truth in the pursuit of a story; cruelty deployed in the process of producing entertainment in the guise of information; and complicity between the fourth estate and the powers of which it is supposed to be a critic.

Nearly everyone has the experience that when we read, see or hear a report of something about which we know the true situation, we find the reporting of it inaccurate and often misleading. The huge increase in the number of 'news' outlets, acres of newsprint, hundreds of broadcast channels, means that there is a demand for 'copy' which goes beyond the capacity of those involved to produce it to any satisfactory standard of competence or accuracy. The natural prurience of the consumer, and the demonstration of Randolph Hearst's doctrine that 'no one ever lost money by underestimating the taste of the public', makes this worse. The damage to the process of government and of reportage is great and growing; the damage to the individuals concerned can be incalculable. News stories are not infrequently obtained by a careful sifting of the contents of a subject's dustbins, a process which has produced one of the more bizarre enterprises of the black economy.

This all suggests, correctly, that even among responsible and well-intentioned journalists and broadcasters there are too many who will fall below expected standards. There are too many pressures of time, lack of specialist expertise, the need to satisfy demanding editors and proprietors (who demand salacious copy, or a new 'angle', rather than accuracy) and the understandable wish to remain employed and be able to pay the mortgage. The problem, and it concerns us directly, is that there is not at present sufficient counterweight to these pressures and influences. Peer group pressures and approval for so many of those working in the media centre upon achieving the meretricious rather than the worthwhile. We do not hear enough the voices of those who themselves set higher standards, and value more substantial achievements. All the more reason for us to encourage Quakers to stay engaged, and to wrestle with the issues of standards.

There is an additional force at work deep in the psyche. It is described by Melanie Klein[12] as the effects of envy leading to a wish to spoil whatever is being achieved by others. Whatever its cause, we can recognise the process all too clearly. It is shown in the way in which our media will build up a personality, and then take delight in knocking them down in public. It is evident in the amoral way in which certain crusading journalists will launch unprincipled attacks on those who in one way or another represent 'authority', using dishonest techniques whilst claiming to be operating from the moral high ground. Klein offers a more timeless example. 'The capacity to give and to preserve life is felt as the greatest gift, and therefore creativeness becomes the greatest cause for envy. The spoiling of creativity implied in envy is illustrated in Milton's *Paradise Lost* where Satan, envious of God, decides to become the usurper of Heaven...This theological idea seems to come down from St Augustine, who describes Life as a creative force opposed to Envy, a destructive force.'[13] And the destructive force of envy is probably only effectively counterbalanced by good example.

If such an example is to be provided, it needs to be done from inside the system as well as outside. If there are enough people within the media, and in government with which it is complicit, who are trying to heal the ills caused by envy, then we may get somewhere. Yet those who remain engaged are no less at risk themselves from the effect of envy. They feel the need to be supported, just as Jacob limped away from his own wrestling bout. That in turn argues for both an understanding by – in our case – the Religious Society as a whole of what is happening, and a sympathy and willingness to uphold those who have this particular Angel in their grasp.

The question of the 'spinning' of news and information lies at the heart of this. We must recognise that it is not only a mote in the eyes of others. After all, the moral equivocation that 'I brief, you leak', 'I explain, you spin' is accepted unthinkingly by most in the media. Yet the need to speak truth to power, and by extension the speaking of truth by power is axiomatic for Quakers, and it is also a given that such speaking shall be plain speaking. Thus question of the presentation of news and information is central to how we engage with the media.

If, in our working situation (or, indeed, in our Quaker enterprises) we have information which we wish or ought to make available to the public, is it enough to do that in an unsubtle, plain-speaking way? Thomas Edison famously claimed that all you have to do is to build a better mousetrap and the world will beat a pathway to your door. We know in practice that it is not enough simply to make a better mousetrap, and wait. First, unless you tell the world convincingly, even persuasively, that you have a better mousetrap, how can they be expected to know, especially amid the background noise of all the other hawkers. Second, unless you make the location of the pathway clear, how will they find you? That is perhaps even more so in the age of the Internet than it has been previously. So you are entitled, are you not, even required to promote your mousetrap? If you then consider the tendencies we have already identified for those responsible for reporting to get it wrong, either by poor standards or deliberate spoiling, then the need to ensure that your presentation over-comes those difficulties becomes all the more pressing. At that moment (and the moment is always present) you face the question whether to set out to 'manage' that supply of information; and if so, what are the limits to be observed.

I have no doubt that to be engaged requires that information and arguments are managed with all due skill. I see no reason to cede the field to those who will use all those techniques, with less scruple, to advance less proper causes. Thus we need in our own dealings to have those among us who are versed in these legiti-mate skills, and to be present among those who so proceed. By skill and by example, we can then maintain the principles and con-sequent limits on how such presentation is made. I believe those principles are five. Never to put forward, whether by commission or omission, information which is false; never to distort information which, although true in itself, will lead the reader or hearer to an intended false conclusion; always to ensure that the fullest possible information is available to support (or, if appropriate, to qualify) the case being presented; to take all possible steps to avoid harm to individuals; and never to allow the end intended to justify unacceptable means of presentation.

The kingdom of the brand

One of the central ways in which concepts are presented or 'spun' is through the use of brands. In the commercial world this is nothing new. The notion of seeking to create loyalty to a branded product through promotional activity was well known to the Quaker chocolate makers. Fry's dominance over Cadbury's and Rowntree's from 1830 to 1860 was at least in part due to their newspaper advertising. When Cadbury introduced its new Cocoa Essence in 1866 it set out to redress the balance by promoting it as 'Absolutely Pure: Therefore Best'.[14] The association of a specific product with a brand name goes back at least as far as 'Hoover' for vacuum cleaner, and probably before.

What are we to make of this? Clearly, if as individuals we participate in the commercial process, we will be citizens of the kingdom of the brand. Indeed, whether we are in business or not, as consumers we cannot escape making choice relating to brands. 'Traidcraft' is no less a brand because it seeks ethical sources for the products it markets under that brand name. We need to accept that branding is a feature of modern commercial life and to go behind the brand to make a judgement about the validity or otherwise of the product itself. It is not my intention in this book and lecture to consider consumer questions in depth. But a reference to them here serves to illustrate that those who wrestle with these issues because they work in business are not doing anything different in kind from the judgements we all have to make as consumers. Thus when I argue that we need to establish a corpus of principles to help those so engaged to make these judgement calls, I hope we may find something of even broader relevance to Quakers who may at first sight consider themselves to be spared this particular dilemma.

Nor is the matter of branding simply for the commercial world. The National Council for Civil Liberties has become *Liberty*, the Spastics Society is now *Scope*, the Labour Party has or had become now *New Labour*. Medical drugs, allied to patents, dazzle by the variety of their branding. Think of all the varieties of aspirin brands. Right across the 'commercial state', the use of brands offers a shorthand term for the aims of an enterprise. Thus even if we are not working in business we need to think through how to deal with the prevalence of branding and whether or not we are justified in deploying it for our own purposes. For the word 'Quaker' is itself in origin simply a brand-name, taken from a term of derision and turned into an identifying label, creating deep emotional attachments.

We should not shrink from exploiting the Quaker brand for good purposes, so long as how we do that is in line with our principles. In media terms, we should make television and radio producers feel that a programme on, say, crime and punishment, is incomplete without a Quaker point of view. In everyday journalism, we should ensure that Quaker thinking is seen as a fertile source of ideas, issues and opinions for the wider press. In politics, we should help politicians to appreciate that Quaker ideas, especially if labelled as such, will enhance both their policies and the value that others will place upon those policies. We should make sure that an event with high salience in current social policy, such as Tim Newell's brilliant Swarthmore Lecture last year, is widely reported, and even anticipated by the media. Lights hidden under bushels have a nasty tendency of going out.

Notes to Chapter 6

1 John Punshon *Portrait in Grey* QHS 1984 p 33
2 George Fox *Journal 1660* pp 499 and 500 of the 1891 Bi-Centenary Edition
3 Sir Richard Body MP in conversation with Tony Stoller 14 December 2000
4 Oxford Research Group Annual Report 1999
5 Philip Ashton *Divided Ideal, The Religious Society of Friends and the Irish Home Rule Controversy 1885–1886* in *The Woodbrooke Journal* Summer 2000
6 Lord Taylor of Gryfe in conversation with Tony Stoller 15 November 2000
7 8 December 2000 p 2
8 Robin Robison in conversation with Tony Stoller 15 October 1999
9 *The Friend* 3 June 1983
10 Gerald Priestland *Priestland Right and Wrong* Fount Paperbacks 1983 p 81
11 Body op. cit.
12 Melanie Klein *Envy and Gratitude and Other Works 1946–1963* The Hogarth Press and the Institute of Psycho-Analysis 1975
13 Ibid. p 202
14 Robert Fitzgerald *Rowntree and the Marketing Revolution 1862–1969* Cambridge, 1995 pp 47–51 quoted in Walvin op. cit. pp 169–70

7   The fire in the thatch

Spiritual values in a secular world

For most of us, the temporal fears are instinctively greater than the spiritual.

> Forgive us, O Lord, we acknowledge ourselves as
>   type of the common man,
> Of the men and women who shut the door and
>   stand by the fire …
> Who fear the hand at the window, the fire in the
>   thatch, the fist in the tavern, the push into the canal …
> Less than we fear the love of God.[1]

Therefore, arguing as I am for a spiritually-based set of principles to govern how we should conduct ourselves in affairs of state or of business is a perilous undertaking. Moreover, if the issue is to be addressed, then a certain amount of 'don't do as I do, do as I tell you' has to be risked. There is also a danger that any attempt will seem obvious, trite or at worst sanctimonious. However, I believe that there is enough bite in our Quaker tradition to make that risk also worth running. The revised *Quaker faith & practice* offers twelve extracts which touch upon the challenges faced by Quakers in the workplace, or more generally in economic affairs[2] and six relating to Friends and the authority of the state.[3] From these, from the rich history of the time when Quakers were more usually engaged with these issues, and from the writings of individual Friends, I will seek to draw out some of the issues for individuals as they wrestle with the problems of engagement.

A Friend who is engaged with the 'commercial state', who wishes to maintain Quaker witness and service and at the same time to be effective in their chosen field, must come to terms with a number of established principles which flow directly from our historic and current traditions. Those principles include offering due obedience to lawful authority, whilst retaining the ability and judgement to challenge authority which is proceeding wrongly; faithfulness and commitment; maintaining Quaker witness, service and testimonies, and keeping and refreshing our faith; personal integrity and trustworthiness. The engaged individual needs to be receptive to the ideas of others, including guidance from fellow Quakers; to sustain a bias against secrecy, in all dealings, but retaining respect for the legitimate privacy of individuals; and to respect the proper dignity of others and themselves, honouring and not abusing friendships at work, avoiding quarrels and showing compassion and good humour. Wrestling with the 'commercial state' involves being resolute in the face of criticism or adversity; speaking plainly and accepting being spoken to plainly by others; welcoming innovation, while not valuing the ephemeral above the tried and tested simply for the sake of novelty; and seeking influence by example rather than by exhortation. It also requires recognising, sustaining and deploying some proper indignation at the follies and misfeasances of the commercial and political worlds. These principles interrelate, and rarely stand alone. Indeed, commonly they will conflict on a particular issue. The essential need is to give each of them appropriate and prayerful consideration as they arise.

Obedience to lawful authority is a concept which often surprises non-Quakers, but is woven deep into the fabric of our Religious Society. Edward Burrough in 1661 wrote of the need to obey legal and state authority in all matters, both actively and passively, but also to resist when anything is commanded of us 'which is not according to equity, justice and a good conscience towards God', putting up with the consequences patiently.[4] That advice, which finds its way also into *Advices and Queries*, stands just as good today and is just as difficult to follow. For the engaged individual, it is generally a support. The rightness of upholding established authority provides a validity for undertaking public work. It is also a valid touchstone for testing when it is right to resist lawful authority. Inevitably, at those times, matters are usually less than straightforward.

There was a story current at the time of the Suez Crisis in 1956 concerning civil servants who had protested about the venture. They were alleged to have been told in so many words that if they were right about the disaster that would overtake the Suez operations then they would be needed to help minimise the damage. If they were wrong, they would never be forgiven if they resigned and undermined the state when British soldiers were fighting overseas.[5] There are echoes of Bright's Alexandrian dilemma here. The lesson is always to test a concern against the principle of qualified respect for the state. There is a clear implication, too, for those who view state authority with automatic disrespect, either because of libertarian principles or out of a dinner-table cynicism. Neither sits well with Quaker practice, which makes a virtue of rendering unto Caesar what is his due.

The challenge is usually even more difficult when it is the other way round, and involves *keeping the faith* against the prevailing trend, or against the demands of authority. For many, this finds its expression in resignation from the enterprise in question, and this can in some situations be a valid reaction, or indeed the only possible response. My interest in this lecture, however, is how those who choose to remain engaged can sustain both their Quaker witness and their practical effectiveness in such circumstances.

It is important to spot the circumstances when keeping faith is paramount, and to try then to act accordingly. Partly, this is a matter of judging where a genuine issue of principle is involved, and when it is not. There are many occasions for the engaged individual in business or in public life when you are touched on a raw nerve. The reaction 'I'm not going to stand for this' needs to be qualified by the prayerful consideration 'unless I really ought to'. We have often seen examples where a principled stand comes at what seems to be the wrong time, over an issue much more minor than others which have passed relatively unchallenged. To get this judgement right is a matter for prayerful reflection even more than for practical consideration. If we are not sure, or even more perhaps if we think we are, these are matters to be opened to the counsel of other Friends, perhaps silently to a Meeting for Worship, or in a more deliberate way through the Clearness techniques.

For keeping faith also involves renewing faith on a constant basis. Engaged Quakers who are not seeking the regular sustenance of Meeting for Worship and of prayer generally are cutting themselves off from the best support system there is. It is an unwelcome paradox that those who are least engaged have the most opportunity to participate in Quaker life and worship. I am fortunate to be able to attend some Tuesday lunchtime Meetings for Worship. Elders there are clear that this is the one Meeting where you are welcome even if late, and where the pressure of taking time out of your working day – rushing in, and usually rushing out again afterwards – is one of the main reasons why the Meeting exists.

All this also requires a substantial level of commitment from each individual Friend. Some of that is time, making time to attend Meeting or space for other Quaker work to which we may be called, despite the appetite of the 'commercial state' for all our waking hours (and some of our sleeping hours, as well). From my own point of view, it means not becoming terminally impatient with the working of our business methods, but committing to trusting the method. One of the central techniques of business or public life is how and when to say 'no', to an invitation to take on some tempting new task. Yet as Quakers, we must commit to saying 'yes' in circumstances where our secular training tells us not to, but where the spirit leads us and will provide the time and effort needed somehow.

If we are to carry our beliefs with us into the 'commercial state', we will also need to come to terms with how much show we will make of them. I have been told that the records of the Great War Tribunals include several instances of Quakers who would not announce that they were Friends, in support of their conscientious objection, because it would unfairly advantage them against others who were asserting an entirely personal pacifism. I can find no such references, but I believe this to be true, and I would like it to be true. At times we all need to be cautioned against making too much of our Quakerism, wearing our beliefs on our sleeve or seeking to exploit them. Equally, there is a risk in making too little of what underpins our faith, especially when hard issues are to be tackled with others. Our colleagues, in business or administration, need to know where we set our limits. They are also entitled to know why. If we have a moral objection to a certain course of action, then the sooner we make that clear the better, especially if the effect of our refusal is to restrict what others are able to do in a common cause. Matthew Parris has even suggested that MPs should be required 'to make free mention of the faith to which [they are] obedient', when this is relevant to an issue on which they are expressing a view.[6]

Trustworthiness and integrity are such obvious concepts, yet so challenging in practice. Any 'motherhood and apple-pie' suspicions here are soon routed by the personal uncertainties of daily life. I am clear that life in Britain generally exhibits these qualities less than it used to. This criticism may be mitigated in part by the realisation that everyone has a slightly different view of exactly where the limits are. What Quakers (and many others) assert is that such limits do exist, and that it is for each individual to try and keep a constant awareness of where they are, and personally to

80

examine each of their actions accordingly. That we will at times fall short in our personal lives is inescapable for most of us. My point here is that those within the 'commercial state' can afford scant slippage, if we are to retain our right to assert that our engagement is principled and for principled ends.

In practice, that means taking Quaker principles of trustworthiness in dealings, and making sure we apply them. Make your yea, yea; and your nay, nay. A word once given, guidance once offered, must not be reneged upon. This means checking when you find yourself reported, and being sure to set the record straight if you have been reported incorrectly. That will often involve quite awkward letters or calls, but it cannot be shirked. If we are dealing with the press, as public life will often require, we will have to judge whether we want simply to set the matter out clearly in private correspondence, or whether we want a public correction. Getting such a correction is rarely automatic, and the process of pursuing it will raise other issues of principle. These may include whether it is ever right to go to law on such occasions; in my view, very rarely and then only very reluctantly.

Trustworthiness also means standing by what we have said, even if inadvertently. I know from experience how great is the temptation to claim that you have been misquoted, or that a remark has been taken out of context. Unless we have been or it has been, then the principle of trustworthiness means that this is a defence we cannot claim. Similarly, if we have given advice and changed our minds, which happens more often than most of us in public administration like to admit, then make sure that we tell those affected, plainly and without artifice.

What is the acid test of integrity? Is it the 'elephant test',[7] in which our integrity stands or falls by the judgement and decision of colleagues and peers? That would suggest that we have behaved with integrity if someone in possession of all the facts decides that we have. Or is it a matter of testing our actions against our knowledge of what is right and wrong, tested in prayer? Since we ourselves rarely know all the facts, least of all about the prejudices which guide us, then we must at the very least submit to the judgement of others whose judgement is soundly based. We also need to be prepared to examine our own actions to test our integrity, both through prayer and by opening them up to other Friends. This was almost institutionalised among Quakers in business or public affairs in past centuries. Surprisingly, although we often ask other Friends in our Meetings on a private, personal basis, there would appear to be very few modern instances of taking such issues to other Quakers collectively or to our established Meetings.

Receptiveness to the ideas of others is another key principle. It should not surprise us. In our own Meetings for Business we seek the right solution not by debate, but encouraging the expression of the will of God by anyone to whom it has been vouchsafed. We try not to repeat a view already expressed, if it aligns with our own, and to be wholly open to the possible rightness of a contrary opinion. In conducting matters in commerce or administration, we should similarly be open to a range of views. More than that, we need also to encourage those who have things to say to speak out, especially if they feel inhibited about offering their opinions as a consequence of the hierarchic traditions of much of the 'commercial state'. As Quakers, we need to be sure that what we do ourselves is best practice, and then to encourage by our example the steady increase of participation.

Openness in all our dealings has been a central concern of the Truth and Integrity in Public Affairs Group. Regarding business dealings, Grigor McClelland has written of justifiable confidentiality in respect of personal data and the right to privacy, competitive tendering, auctions and negotiation and price-sensitive information. He contrasts this with unjustifiable secrecy and deception such as suppressing information harmful to commercial interests, distorted product promotion and breaches of trust.[8] This is a more helpful approach than the outright condemnation of any forms of secrecy as it points up the tensions which exist between the right to know and the right to enjoy proper privacy.

The most satisfactory approach for an engaged Quaker seems to be to start the examination of each issue with a predisposition towards openness. In public administration and government in particular, that ought to mean that information is made fully available unless there are strong reasons for not doing so, and that those strong reasons will need to be tested against the default position which is to make things public. In affairs of state, it will usually only be the risk of real harm which will justify overturning open assumptions. The extraordinary strains of the opposite outcome are related by Sir John Colville in his diary account of the press conspiring to keep secret the incapacity of a prime minister, as happened for several weeks in late June and early July 1953, when Churchill's secret stroke left his private secretaries in *de facto* charge of the country.[9] In commercial matters, the public interest on questions such as safety or environmental damage should always override business self-interest. A Quaker in a position of influence in either of these fields will be driven by our principles to influence organisations in that direction. The value of having that influence from within is likely to make the better contribution towards achieving the goal of openness. We need to recognise the reality that protests, launched from outside an organisation, usually generate extra defensiveness in the enterprise being challenged, and thus make the release of information harder to achieve.

Each individual's right to *privacy* is an important counterbalance. In business, a company may often be able to deflect criticism of itself by pointing the finger at one of its employees. Even if they are indeed responsible for some failing, they have a right to confidentiality which requires proper respect. Employers usually have a legal obligation of confidentiality towards their employees, for example regarding disciplinary actions. I believe that we should defend that right even when it means a company or organisation having to endure attack which might be unjustified. That is even more the case when an individual is blameless (which means that blame has not been established, whether or not it is suspected). I have written already of the dubious pleasure taken by sections of the media in 'exposing' individuals, who may later well be found to have been entirely innocent. Even if they do carry some blame, the pain of public humiliation may well be out of all proportion to the error or omission concerned, and as managers or employers Quakers need to be zealous in protecting the privacy of individuals.

Respect for the dignity of individuals involved with us in the 'commercial state', or those affected by its processes, is another fundamental principle. Management theory coach Tom Peters observed in one of his training speeches that, in a good organisation, there is a mental sign in the bosses' minds that says 'Tyranny has no place here'. No one should be frightened to come to work because of how they fear they will be treated. Our role is not only to avoid such practices, it is also to set an example that good management should never require a raised voice, either literally or metaphorically. We need at all times to be sensitive to the dignity of our staff, our colleagues and even our superiors. Compassion is one of the most important of management qualities. That respect also needs to be given to people at all ranks within an enterprise. I have written already about the importance of encouraging ideas to be put forward by everyone involved with a matter, and giving proper consideration to those ideas. The same point applies in how we treat people in an organisation. Here again, the example which we should be setting as Quakers will be at least as important as whether we ourselves measure up to our own standards in this respect.

One of the pleasures of being part of a corporate enterprise are the friendships we make. They are on many levels, sometimes deep and lifelong, sometimes pleasant acquaintance while our paths run alongside each other. Respect for the dignity of individuals also means not abusing those friendships. We are not entitled to expect or ask for favours, nor to give them improperly. This can be a stern test. There is a fine line between, say, the kindness of warning a friend of an impending problem and improperly exploiting that relationship by providing access to private information. This is again a matter where an individual instance needs to be tested against at times conflicting principles. In all questions of personal relationships and respect for individuals, the best safeguard of all is good humour, to walk cheerfully over the world. And as well as taking up Fox's maxim, we could also do worse than follow Yeats' advice, never but in merriment to begin a quarrel.[10] The value of good humour cannot be overstated, nor can the willingness to say sorry when needed.

In so many ways we are required to be *resolute and competent*, firm in a purpose which we judge to be proper and despite 'what is inflicted on us'.[11] That applies not just to the traditional areas of Quaker activity but also as we engage with the 'commercial state'. Like Jacob with the Angel, we need to keep a firm hold on our purpose, even when we suffer damage as a result. Once again, though, applying this principle needs care. Being steadfast in a false cause is simple obstinacy. The point is to test one's own judgement with prayer and with advice. I have just written of the value of good humour. I set a high store also by proper indignation. If we do not feel worked up about a number of things which manifest themselves in business practice, in public administration, even in our Religious Society, then we haven't been paying attention! Such indignation, properly and prayerfully challenged, can have almost as much effect in moving mountains as the proverbial faith. The epitaph on Jonathan Swift's tomb in St Patrick's Cathedral in Dublin reads 'where savage indignation can no longer tear at his heart'.[12] It is clear, then, what drove Swift to preach and to satirise and to reform.

Competence does not sit as comfortably among Friends as it should, nor as it did in our history. The parable of the talents[13] amply supports the efficiencies demanded by nineteenth century

Quaker enterprises, and which underpinned their careful business practices and thrifty innovation. Because so much of our experience through individual Quakers now comes from outside the managerial world, we too often run the risk of 'opting out into woolliness' in David Shutt's memorable phrase.[14]

As Quakers we pride ourselves on *plain speaking*. Yet even this basic tenet of how we try to live our lives is qualified in practice. We also seek to avoid causing pain to others by what we say, and the result is not infrequently that we fail to say something that ought to be said. In dealing with the 'commercial state', plain speaking is an important principle, but once more it is one to be tested in each circumstance. At the moment of disengagement, especially if you have resigned or withdrawn in a fairly high-profile circumstance, you may have an opportunity to speak your mind. If this is on a supposedly newsworthy matter, then what you say may even be quite widely reported. Yet too many such gestures, often made at great personal cost, tend to be nine-day wonders, soon replaced by the next 'story'. For those who remain engaged, the problem is closer to that which we may all feel in a particularly sluggish Preparative Meeting. Is this the right time to upset whomever by making plain what they will find unpalatable? Medieval kings kept jesters by them, a Fool allowed licence to tell them the uncomfortable truth without (usually) suffering the standard penalty of the messenger bringing bad news. In this lecture, I am conscious that I am taking to myself some of the Fool's privilege.

For I judge that one of the ways in which we currently fall below the standards set by Quakers in the past is in our unwillingness to speak plainly, especially to those in power, from within the 'commercial state'. We have no such reluctance from outside, but then that is the obvious role of dissenters, and though it may often be physically uncomfortable it offers a clear sense of moral snugness. If we are saying in the councils of power what is being shouted from outside the gates, our level of discomfort is of altogether a different order. Yet it needs to be done when it needs to be done. Bear in mind that speaking truth to power does not mean showing disrespect, provoking a quarrel (even on a professional level) or setting out to cause pain. It should always be accompanied by due courtesy. The Declaration to Charles II which sets out our Peace Testimony is a model of respectful phrasing.[15] But if we wish to remain engaged, then we have to accept the burden of plain speaking just as much now as in 1660.

Since we claim the privilege of plain speaking to others, we must welcome it when they speak plainly to us. In many aspects of our lives we have got out of the habit of robust debate, conducted with passion but without rancour. That also won't do. Clear and unadorned speech and writing has the immense benefit of being open to all, and encouraging participation. If we are to gain those advantages in our work within the 'commercial state' (and elsewhere as well, not least within the Religious Society) then we must be prepared for our own plain speaking to be replied to in the same terms, and our obfuscations challenged and shown up. We need also as individuals to be fairly heedless of what our ego will tell us is our reputation. We should be very reluctant indeed to conclude that we have been defamed in such a way that we need to seek legal redress. That should be true even when the uncomfortably common technique of the professional or personal 'smear campaign' is used against us or against a cause we support. Every privilege brings a corresponding obligation. With the privilege of plain speaking comes the obligation to put up with what they say about us, particularly when it is unfair, with as much good humour as we can muster.

Welcoming innovation is a version of the advice we are given to live adventurously. Again there is a creditable Quaker business tradition of adopting new methods. Joseph Fry's successes in chocolate manufacturing, soap boiling and printing owed much to the fact that he 'was a good chemist and did much to improve the articles he manufactured.'[16] In Coalbrookdale, the Quaker iron-

87

masters were notable for their technological innovations, for example through the success of the Ironbridge Works in establishing cast iron as a usable material for construction which 'introduced a new era in structural design of all kinds'. The work of the Rowntrees in York combined technical advance in the manufacturing of chocolate with social innovation. Their initiatives were designed 'to make employees feel that they are more than mere parts of an industrial machine' [17] and before 1914 they were 'remarkably unusual and far-sighted'.

That obligation stays with us today. We need to be receptive to innovations, technological, social or political. In the time of the applicability of Moore's law, [18] we are likely to have no shortage of new ideas to deal with. If we greet them enthusiastically, though, we should not do so uncritically. As the 'commercial state' continues its fascination with what new technology can achieve, we need to be active in encouraging new ideas. Yet we also should be careful and thorough in ensuring that we do not discard a tried method until we are sure that its replacement is of genuine worth and not just a fashionable chimera.

In all of these principles for the individual engaging with the 'commercial state' we should be seeking to *influence others by the example of our witness*, not by preaching. Secular society as a whole seems to be going through an exhortatory phase. Time and again, in business life and in public affairs we are asked to accept that something is so because it is said to be so. New technologies are established, therefore it is claimed that social or commercial change will follow automatically. It won't. Change comes about because people as a whole alter their behaviour when presented with an opportunity; or does not happen because they decline to do so. We can now carry out our food shopping entirely over the Internet. Until people do so in large numbers, this is a potential revolution not an actual one.

Let us avoid believing that we can make things happen simply by asserting that they should (or are). Our tradition is one of service which provides witness. If we are to engage effectively with the 'commercial state' from within, that is our surest tool. Let them judge what we are by what we do, however challenging that may be for each individual. And let them be influenced to consider our way of doing things by seeing the effect it has when we follow it. That was the great impact of the Quaker traders of the eighteenth and nineteenth centuries, and it is the opportunity and challenge which now faces those among us who remain within the commercial and administrative sectors of our society.

Notes to Chapter 7

1 T.S. Eliot *Murder in the Cathedral* Part II
2 *Quaker faith & practice* 1995 sections 23.53–23.62
3 *Quaker faith & practice* 1995 sections 23.86–23.91
4 Edward Burrough, 1661 in *Quaker faith & practice* 1995, section 23.86
5 Quoted in Donald Cameron-Watt's review of *Whitehall and the Suez Crisis*, ed. Kelly and Gorst; *New Statesman* 1 April 2000 p 58
6 Matthew Parris Parliamentary Sketch *The Times* 8 December 2000 p 2
7 It is said that two philosophers were competing how most accurately and completely to describe an elephant. One produced many densely argued pages. The other won by saying simply 'I know it when I see it'.
8 Grigor McClelland *Truth and Integrity in Business* included in *Questions of Integrity* London Yearly Meeting 1993 pp 49–66
9 Sir John Colville *The Fringes of Power* volume two Sceptre 1987 pp 328–30
10 W.B. Yeats *Prayer for my Daughter*
11 Burrough op. cit.

12 *Ubi saeva indignation ulterius cor lacerare nequit*
13 Matthew 25: 14–30
14 Lord Shutt of Greetland in conversation with Tony Stoller, 29 November 2000
15 Raistrick op. cit. p 215
16 Ibid. p 142
17 Asa Briggs *Social Thought and Social Action: A study of the work of Seebohm Rowntree 1871–1954* London 1961, quoted in Walvin op. cit. p 203
18 see page 14

8 Passing over Jabbok

Implications of engagement for our Religious Society

This has been a long journey, this venture into the challenging land over the Jabbok, and one from which I have learnt a great deal. I now need to reach a conclusion, or at least a resolution. What I have discerned about the way we live now, and the dilemmas which confront Quakers engaged in business and administrative life, has confirmed me in my view that we need to engage the 'commercial state' to a much greater extent than we currently do. I have found, as I expected, that there is much of interest and value in the commercial and political worlds which we in our Religious Society could use much better. We could also valuably learn what of this to discard. In particular, we have sound Quaker principles, firmly in line with our tradition and inspirations, which can guide the individual who is so engaged.

We need to return at least in part to our witness in the worlds of politics and business, which we used to offer but do so no longer. To achieve that, we need to change in the way we think, how we respond to the engaged people among us, and how we conduct our Quaker affairs, in order to make possible a partnership between Friends engaged with the 'commercial state' and the rest of our Religious Society.

First and foremost, we need to re-examine and change our prejudice against the 'commercial state' and, by (unintended) implication, our undervaluing of those engaged with it. You may ask whether there is any such prejudice. I have found that there is, and that feeling is shared by many currently 'engaged' Quakers. As so often, it is the unintended use of language which gives away our true assumptions. Speaking to a Monthly Meeting seminar, a well-respected weighty Friend – after ascertaining that thirty or so of the forty Friends present were working or had worked in education – observed that 'Friends assume that no one is in something awful like business'.

Those from the caring professions dominate membership. It was estimated in 1989 that half of all British Quakers are or were professionally involved in this type of work.[1] Around one third are or were teachers.[2] It would be surprising if their encounters with the violation of ethical and social principles, by enforced exposure to the 'market', had left them comfortable with the 'commercial state'. (In fact, what they have endured is usually a gross distortion of what best commercial experience could offer.) Yet there is also a general feeling among Friends which recoils from involvement with the commercial world. The effect of this 'chill factor' is that only a small percentage of members or attenders come from that sector of employment, which is far and away the largest sector in our society as a whole. Of course this is my value judgement, but if you require hard evidence, look around you at your own Meeting.

Second, I hope that we can start to demonstrate a growing feeling of comfort in engaging with the 'commercial state' by conducting our own Quaker affairs, where they interface with it, with more confidence, competence and commitment.

As a start, we need to accept and embrace the image of Quakers held by a good number of those in the wider world. They believe that we have a voice which deserves to be heard on the key social and political issues of our day. I have even heard it said (in a most inappropriate phrase) that 'Quakers punch above their weight' on public affairs. And indeed public administration is perhaps a natural sector of resort for Quakers. The possibility of undertaking some public service whilst being gainfully and interestingly employed is a neat matching of personal ambition and moral duty. Despite that, and the number of Quakers so engaged, the Religious Society is institutionally uneasy with political engagement. We should give our Parliamentary work a more central position within the main tasks of service and witness, and try to position the Religious Society as a natural source of membership for major Public Inquiries or advisors.

Is such 'positioning' proper, let alone desirable? Of course it is, if it is done in a proper way and for proper ends, so let us stop using the alibi of caution as an excuse for inaction. Let Friends House find the will and the money to establish a press and media post to provide the voice box with which we can effectively speak truth to power.

Let us help *The Friend* to return to a position of significance in our witness, becoming essential reading for more than just the news, announcements and letters pages. Here is an independent journal with a respected tradition and a reputation which goes beyond Quaker circles. It should serve both as a genuine forum for debate within the Religious Society (and all the more reason then to ensure that it retains its independence) and as a medium for the communication of Quaker ideas and ideals to a wider world hungry for such a lead. In any truly democratic structure, independent and responsible journalism plays an essential part. *The Friend* and the Religious Society are entitled to have the highest expectations of each other. Those responsible for *The Friend* need to accept that their responsibility goes further than simply survival. Indeed, they will do that so much more easily if they make it possible for the magazine to offer good and compelling content. And the Religious Society as a whole, and especially those who hold responsibilities for our 'corporate work', must welcome the challenge and scrutiny which such content will bring. It is a sign of a healthy and self-confident organisation that it encourages criticism and is unafraid of it.

In the conduct of our own business affairs, let us become comfortable with the handling of money, resources and staff issues, in an ethical way, and let Friends participate widely in these tasks. If we are tentative, feeling that we are somehow in alliance with Mammon, we will produce outcomes which are neither effective, fair to the individuals concerned, nor morally satisfactory. So let us seek out, to a much greater degree than we now do, those within the Religious Society whose skills lie in these fields and involve them to work where they are the best able. That may mean other Friends ceding place from time to time, but this is a common enterprise needing the varied skills of all of us.

Third, it is high time we took a hard look at our preoccupation with structures, to the exclusion of both prayer and action. Do not, under any circumstances, give this task to another working party! I estimate that, during my first four years' service on a Central Committee, eighty per cent of our time has been spent on corporate reorganisation, committee names, five year plans, objectives, mission statements and the like. I am by trade a bureaucrat, and yet it appals me. What must it do for 'normal' people?

I urge on Yearly Meeting and our Religious Society a self-denying ordinance, a moratorium on *any* consideration of committee structures, corporate witness organisation or more than the essential minimum of business and management planning, for three years. Let us neither make nor consider any new changes in our Quaker enterprises, but try and do the best, in worship and in service, with what we now have. Of course it is imperfect, but it always will be. And when we come to change (or if, as I fear, we persist in structural preoccupations) then let us take only the best of the techniques of the 'commercial state', not just the most fashionable, most intricate and those that use the most paper. Let us seek to understand the principles which we are planning to adopt, and then interpret and implement them in the way that best suits our purpose, not just a slavish imitation of what we have seen in a different context. A recent letter to *The Friend* asks where is our version of Gerry Robinson, to 'sort us out'.[3] As I have written above, he/she/they are among us, waiting to be asked. At the right time, let us ask them.

Fourth, how can we encourage Friends to wrestle with the Angel of the 'commercial state'? And how can we bring others who are so engaged, many of whom feel close to the ideas and ideals of Quakerism, to appreciate that the Religious Society has a place for them?

Most of all, as I have already discussed, we need a shift in our own attitudes. Next, we need to look at the practical arrangements of our Meetings for Worship. Preparative Meetings can usefully target some Meetings for Worship at times and in places which fit the timetables of the workplace. Central Committees need to plan their own activities in such a way that busy people are more readily able to participate. The future health and growth of Britain Yearly Meeting will depend at least in part on attracting some active members from outside the caring professions and from those in routine work. That will mean making their participation possible by the simple expedient of doing it at times and in places when they can take part.

Local and central Meetings may also consider whether they really offer the opportunities for engaged individuals to test their concerns and review their actions. That may mean having in place the mechanisms to assist 'clearness', and taking the initiative to offer them in this context, rather than only for personal emotional or spiritual crises. When was the last time your Meeting gave this type of issue prayerful consideration? Yet unless engaged Quakers see their proper preoccupations receiving such attention, how can they be encouraged to value what they do and to bring such matters to Meeting for its scrutiny and support? A hundred years ago, Friends did this routinely. Nowadays, they do it hardly at all. Nor are our Meetings much involved in the industrial missions which many churches offer to those in the workplace. Virtually without exception, those Quakers I have spoken with who are distinguished in the 'commercial state' feel that, whilst their personal faith has sustained them, they have received no support worth speaking of from the Religious Society, often through decades of public service.

There are real problems posed by the supposedly pivotal role of Monthly Meeting. We know that many Friends feel distanced from these Meetings, yet they continue to have a pivotal role in our church government and for communication between 'outlying' Friends and the 'centre'. This mechanism has an inbuilt bias against the participation of those fully engaged with the 'commercial state', or indeed busy Friends generally. Monthly Meetings are long and diffuse. They take up a good deal of the spare time available to most working Friends, and can be accessed in practice only by attendance. For so long as they remain the main channel of communication between the accessibility and vitality of Preparative Meetings and the 'corporate work' of the Religious Society as a whole, then such contact will be at best slight. I am not (here) suggesting a change in the structure of Monthly Meetings, nor (at this stage) in Meeting for Sufferings, which suffers similar handicaps, because the last thing we need is to spend more time now on structures. But I do strongly urge a change in our perception of which channels represent the most effective communication within the Religious Society.

If we want Friends as a whole to know what is being done on their behalf we need to be much better at telling them about it. We need to demonstrate a genuine and pro-active openness with all of our central work, and for those so engaged to embrace that bias towards transparency. If we want to use the skills and contacts of individual Friends who are not part of Central Committees, then we need to encourage them to respond on the basis of that knowledge, and for their response to be welcome, welcomed and acted upon. This does not need yet another round of structural changes, or at least not yet. We need to let form follow function naturally, not to try again to engineer it when the fundamental preconceptions have not changed. Let us help attitudes to shift, then take such small steps as seem of practical use to meet specific needs, and the rest will follow.

The goal of such inclusiveness should be to re-establish a partnership between those Friends who are engaged and have influence in the 'commercial state' and those in the caring professions and/or committed to direct action. Together, fortified by faith and Quaker practices, we can return the Religious Society to a position of consistent relevance to at least some of the great social, political and economic issues of our day. To do that, we must encourage some Friends at least to return to their once traditional involvement with business and political affairs. Otherwise, we will dwindle in numbers, in relevance, and eventually even in our self-regard. Quietism in this respect, as in others, is not a virtue, particularly if it is unduly prolonged. Indeed, as any group becomes more self-obsessed it risks subsiding into a mere sect. (There are uncomfortable parallels between our unwillingness to participate in business or in public affairs and our reluctance to engage ecumenically.)

Part of any new inclusiveness will involve also making ourselves open to membership and attendance from those who are already so engaged, and who seek a religious and moral underpinning for the work they are doing and the standards they seek to bring to that work. We need to establish a climate for such participation. That will mean making engaged people feel welcome, opening our structures to them, bringing their techniques in to the appropriate areas of our own work and being clear about those areas where the religious must replace the secular. We will need to show that the Religious Society has the mechanisms to provide them with support for what they do, and ways to test the validity of their concerns and actions. Let us embrace and build upon initiatives such as the Quakers in Business Group, making this type of activity central rather than peripheral to our current concerns and work.

For much of the second half of the past century, Quakers in Britain have sought to escape from the implications of the material world in favour of the 'ethical', the caring and the simply nice. This has led our Religious Society away from institutional involvement with the 'commercial state' at the very time that this entity has come to have the greatest influence over our societies as a whole. Our distaste for the material world has led us to undervalue the contribution made by those who engage the 'commercial state' to the point where we no longer enjoy much participation from them nor – as a direct consequence – a proper understanding of the skills they can offer or the techniques of which we could avail ourselves. As we enter the twenty-first century, we have the opportunity to redress the imbalance between our support for those who dissent and those who are engaged within the system.

We have among us, and should want to have more, those who have crossed the Jabbok and are wrestling with the Angel which is the 'commercial state'. It is at times an unequal struggle. Seeking to emulate Jacob, though, they try to cling on until they receive an outcome, a blessing. In doing so, they may well endure damage and injury to themselves. But what they are doing is of value and deserves encouragement, support and at times emulation. To withhold such support because of a Stoical suspicion of the 'commercial state' is a spiritual as well as a practical failure. As the religious genius of Spanish Jewry, Nahmanides, wrote in the thirteenth century, the Stoic with his disdain for the material world 'is like a man who has backed out of a room but will not turn round. And behind his back is God.'[4]

Notes to Chapter 8

1   Ben Pink Dandelion *The need for adult religious learning in Britain Yearly Meeting* p 87 in *Searching the Depths: essays on being a Quaker today* ed. Harvey Gillman and Alastair Heron QHS 1996

2   1988 QSRE Conference of Education. Paper by Peter Fishpool, quoted in *Searching the Depths* op. cit.

3   *The Friend* 20 October 2000 p 16

4   *Torat Ha'Adam (The Law of Man)* Nahmanides, quoted in *Kaddish* Leon Wieseltier Picador 1998 p 15

Acknowledgements and disclaimers

The opinions I have expressed in these pages, and will do again in the lecture which this book accompanies, are entirely my own. They do not seek to represent the views of my current employer, The Radio Authority, nor of my former employer, John Lewis plc. What I have written about ethical investment is entirely my own view, not that of Friends Provident nor of my colleagues on the Committee of Reference for the Stewardship Funds, on which I serve. To put my comments on *The Friend* into context, I must record that my wife works for the magazine, but what I have written is my opinion and not hers.

I am indebted to all the people who gave me their time and their views. Some of them did not know, when they spoke to me, that this was to be grist for a Swarthmore Lecture, and to them I offer not only my thanks but also my apologies for what was thought a necessary secrecy (see chapter 4!). They include Mary Ashwin, Michael Bartlett, Richard Body, Roland Carn, Richard Hooper, Jim Malcolmson, Roger Morton, Sally Richards, Robin Robison, Henry Ruff, David Shutt, Heather Swailes, Tom Taylor and John Whitney. A group of Friends from Southampton – Frank Boulton, Terry Hawton, David Heathfield and Frank Goh – gave their time, wisdom, disagreement where necessary, and patient guidance, encouraging me to find and embrace the concept of 'partnership', and I am most grateful to them and to my PM as a whole, as I am to the Friends House Library staff. I offer a word of apology, too, to those I did not speak with. Although I set off to do some comprehensive research, I soon realised that this had to be largely my own thoughts, not a compendium of others.

Margaret Heathfield and Gil Skidmore guided me through this project most skilfully, mixing support and prodding in due measure and at the right times. I felt their support throughout, I

100

feel it still, and I am most appreciative. I am grateful also for agreement from Lyn Wilson and Roland Carn to quote from unpublished sources, to the John Lewis Partnership for permission to reproduce extracts from *The Gazette*, and generally to my present and past employers for agreement to use material.

None of the above, of course, bear any responsibility for errors or daft opinions, which are all entirely my own.

To all those who gave help in darker times, and to my family, to whom this book and lecture are dedicated, I offer endless thanks, which are still insufficient.

Tony Stoller
Southampton, February 2001

Select Bibliography

HISTORY

On the assumption that other than Quakers may use this bibliography, the standard Quaker history is *Portrait in Grey* by John Punshon (QHS 1984). Christopher Hill's *A Turbulent, Seditious and Factious People* (Oxford University Press 1988) covers the social, political and religious events of the seventeenth century from which Quakerism emerged. For a review of Quakers in commerce and industry, Arthur Raistrick, *Quakers in Science and Industry* (Sessions Book Trust, York 1950, in the 1993 edition) is the first port of call, with *The Quakers, Money and Morals* by James Walvin (John Murray 1997) following closely behind. Alastair Heron's *Quakers in Britain, a Century of Change* (Curlew Graphics, Kelso, Scotland 1995) has more substance than its slight appearance suggests.

Margaret Forster's *Rich Desserts and Captain's Thin* (Vintage 1997) wonderfully evokes the story of the Quaker biscuit-making family, the Carrs of Carlisle. Sir John Colville's two volumes of diaries *The Fringes of Power* (Hodder and Stoughton 1985) give a compelling picture of the workings of the highest levels of government during and after the Second World War, and the society vanishing with it. A bleaker perspective is provided by Alan Bullock, *Hitler and Stalin: Parallel Lives* (HarperCollins 1991) and by Eric Hobsbawm's *Age of Extremes, The Short Twentieth Century* (Michael Joseph 1994). The interplay between Friends and the events in Germany before and during the Second World War is set out in *Quakers and Nazis; Inner Light in Outer Darkness* by Hans A Schmitt (Missouri University Press 1997).

SOCIETY TODAY AND TOMORROW

I liked the analysis of the state of the nation provided by Andrew Marr's *Ruling Britannia* (Michael Joseph 1995) when it first came out, and have only slightly revised my opinion downwards since. Otherwise, you can take your pick of the futurologists and their analysis of the present. Charles Handy in *The Empty Raincoat* (Hutchinson 1995), Charles Leadbetter in *Living on Thin Air* (Penguin Books 2000) and Will Hutton in *The State We're In* (Vintage 1996) are all thought-provoking. The best current view of the Internet is in John Naughton's *A Brief History of the Future* (Phoenix 1999), and of the economic future is in Hamish McRae's *The World in 2020* (HarperCollins 1994). I also recommend *The Economist*'s publication, *The World in 2000*. For a regulator's view of how television may be regulated, *Deciding What We Watch* by Colin Shaw (Oxford University Press 1999) represents a fascinating overview.

The publications of the Oxford Research Group always repay study. In particular, *Weapons Decision: Proposals for an Informed Parliament* (October 1996) and *Collective Security: A New Role for Britain* (March 2000) are current reports relating to my themes.

QUAKER AND OTHER PERSPECTIVES
In additional of course to the indispensable *Quaker faith & practice* (Britain Yearly Meeting 1995), I have spent time reading and re-reading many of my predecessors as Swarthmore Lecturers. Two are quoted in my text: Margaret Heathfield, *Being Together* (QHS 1994), Jonathan Dale, *Beyond the Spirit of the Age* (QHS 1996). Ben Pink Dandelion's thesis, published as *A Sociological Analysis of the Theology of Quakers* (Edwin Mellen Press 1996) is a valuable source-book. *Searching the Depths, Essays in Being a Quaker Today*, edited by Harvey Gillman and Alastair Heron (QHS 1996) compiles one range of themes; *Questions of Integrity* (London Yearly Meeting 1993) another. *Priestland Right and Wrong* by Gerald Priestland (Collins 1983) is an individual view of some of these matters. *Quakers in Politics: Pragmatism or Principle* by Jo Vallentine and Peter D. Jones (Australia Yearly Meeting 1990) shows that these concerns are not only British.

Dietrich Bonhoeffer's *Ethics* (in translation SCM Press 1995) is remarkable as a Christian work and much more. Ideas on Jewish themes were provoked by *Kaddish* by Leon Wieseltier (Picador 1999).

Back again with Quaker practice, the study pack *Is your money working for the world?* compiled by Jennie Levin (Joseph Rowntree Charitable Trust 2001) is a comprehensive working guide for individuals and groups. The Quakers and Business Group has just published *Good Business: Ethics at Work* (2000), and for a full perspective these two perhaps need to be read together. Our business methods are described and analysed in *Mind the Oneness* by Robert Halliday (QHS 1991).

WEBSITES

The Britain Yearly Meeting site is www.quaker.org.uk
Websites providing information on ethical investment include
Friends Provident at www.friendsprovident.co.uk/stewardship/policy
the UK Social Investment Forum at www.uksif.org the Ethical
Investment Co-operative at www.ethicalinvestment.org.uk and the
research body Eiris at www.eiris.org
The Oxford Research Group is at www.oxfordresearchgroup.org
Public Concern at Work, the 'whistleblowing' lobby group, have
a site at www.pcaw.demon.co.uk Further details on the radio
licensing activities referred to in Chapter 4 can be found at
www.radioauthority.org.uk The Jubilee 2000 Coalition's site is
www.jubilee2000.org

Views on this lecture, or further questions, may be addressed to
www.swarthmorelecture2001@yahoo.com

5 March 2001